Immigration and the Legalization of Racism

Lisa Marie Jakubowski

Fernwood Publishing · Halifax

Editing: Brenda Conroy
Cover illustration: Barrie Maguire
Design and production: Beverley Rach
Printed and bound in Canada by: Hignell Printing Limited

A publication of:
Fernwood Publishing
Box 9409, Station A
Halifax, Nova Scotia
B3K 5S3

Fernwood Publishing Company Limited gratefully acknowledges the financial support of the Ministry of Canadian Heritage and the Nova Scotia Department of Education and Culture.

Canadian Cataloguing in Publication Data

Jakubowski, Lisa Marie, 1965-
Immigration and the legalization of racism.

Includes bibliographical reference
ISBN 1-895686-74-1

1. Canada -- Race relations. 2. Racism -- Canada. 3. Emigration and immigration law -- Canada. I. Title.

FC104.J34 1997   305.8'00971   C97-950034-6
F1035.A1J34 1997

In loving memory of my Baba, Mary Gutt.
Her spirit, like a precious star,
will forever guide me.

Contents

Acknowledgements

I would like to express my appreciation to those individuals whose support and assistance facilitated the completion of this project. Many thanks are offered to Harry Glasbeek, Carl James, Norene Pupo and Richard Weisman for their helpful comments and suggestions on earlier versions of this book. For creating such a supportive and stimulating intellectual environment within which to work, I am grateful to my colleagues, students and the staff of Brescia College. Thank you also to the Social Sciences and Humanities Research Council of Canada (SSHRC) for financially endorsing this research in its earlier form. Finally, to Errol Sharpe, Brenda Conroy, Beverley Rach and the rest of the staff at Fernwood Publishing, I extend my sincere appreciation for so supportively and enthusiastically undertaking this project.

On a more personal note, I wish to acknowledge the support and friendship of Carol Duncan, Mary-Jo Nadeau and Dwaine Plaza who very selflessly shared their intellectual insights and resources with me. Beyond the intellectual, Carol, Mary-Jo and Dwaine were always available with emotional support through those particularly stressful and isolating periods of research and writing. Thanks to each one of these true friends for being there.

I am forever grateful to my family for their everlasting belief in me. To my parents, Anne and Stefan, and my brother and sister-in-law, Rob and Marie, thank you for your love and support, for tolerating my moods and for understanding my many absences. For brightening each and every one of my days, I extend an extra-special thank you to my precious niece, Stefanie Christine.

Last, but certainly not least, I remain eternally indebted to my mentor, colleague and friend, Livy Visano. Throughout our various intellectual journeys together, I continue to be challenged and inspired by Livy's invaluable insights. This, in combination with his sensitivity and his immeasurable support and loyalty, make for a remarkable collegial relationship. Livy Visano is a very gifted and rare educator and scholar with whom it is truly a privilege to work.

Foreword

Somehow it seems appropriate to be writing this foreword to Lisa Jakubowski's *Immigration and the Legalization of Racism* on Canada Day.

My morning newspaper's headlines and letters to the editor wax about Canada's fine achievements: its abundance, the wealth of opportunities that it affords and the pride we have in our tolerance, our diversity, our multiculturalism, our reputation for decency, our love for peace and our peacekeeping. The newspaper also carries a special laudatory article on the judiciary, on its independence, sagacity, open-mindedness and fairness.

July 1, 1996 has provided yet another occasion to celebrate the oft-repeated characterization of Canada as a mature liberal-capitalist democracy. Politicians and opinion-makers purport to see Canada as a nation state which, while economically wedded to wealth creation by private profit-making activities, adheres to a model of political equality. The rights of people stem from the fact that each person is considered the legal equal of any other person. Accordingly, neither governments nor private sector actors are to be allowed to offer or to deny opportunities, entitlements and benefits on any basis that negates this equality. Only rational criteria, based on consensually agreed upon norms, permit differential treatment. For instance, employment opportunities and rights are to be decided by reference to criteria based on efficient production, not on criteria such as family relationships, gender or race. In sum, as much as possible, rights and privileges are not to depend on power, but on reason. In the legal setting, this is given effect by demanding adherence to Dicey's concept of the Rule of Law.

That the law applies equally to all, then, is a given. Of course, the law itself is not to be biased in such a way so that its equal application might favour some members of society over others. And while, in theory, our electoral system, with its notion of a sovereign parliament, might produce laws with this kind of bias, the maturity of the Canadian liberal democracy is said to be demonstrated by its establishment of a series of inhibitions on majoritarian law-making. Human Rights Acts forbid governments and private power-wielding actors from making decisions on "irrational" grounds, such as family relationships, sex, sexual orientation, age, gender, political belief, nationality, ethnicity, race and the like. The Charter of Rights and Freedoms forbids government from making discriminatory laws or decisions. We Canadians explicitly have told our wealth owners and governments that there is to be no conduct, nor law, that discriminates on proscribed grounds. This and our cosy relationship with the United States (as well as our military impotence) have given us the confidence and the self-asserted claim to the necessary status to seek to occupy the international high ground. We offer ourselves as international brokers and peacekeepers. This flattering self-portrayal, which is rarely questioned, is problematized by Lisa

Jakubowski's book. It does so by interrogating our immigration laws and policies.

Immigration law provides a fertile field for such an investigation. It is here that Canadians are directly confronted by people whom they see as "others." Immigrants and refugees are not just "others"; they are "others" who might make demands on us, who might diminish our wealth, who might take away our jobs. Our principles of tolerance and non-discrimination are put to the test. Immigration law and policy is where our liberal-democratic aspirations which centre on social and political equality meet head-on with our capitalist goals which are preoccupied with the maintenance of economic inequality.

Canada is a land of migrants precisely because, as a capitalist economy, it has been unable to generate enough labour to meet its labour market requirements. The question of where these migrants are to come from is not decided by the logic of capitalism. This logic's thrust is that, as labour requirements go up or down, there ought to be policies that can satisfy those needs as cheaply and as efficiently as possible from a capitalist's perspective. It is arguable that it is this logic that has led to the racial and ethnic diversity of Canada's modern population.

Lisa Jakubowski shows that, initially, the idea was to build a white Canada, preferably from British and Northern European stock. This idea was based on prejudices spawned by British imperialists and made part of the elite's culture in Canada. The unsatisfied need for labour and the rise of internationalism put an end to this white Canada policy by 1962 (and to the very similarly-based Australian policy by 1972). But, historically generated fears, loathings and popular cultures do not go away merely because they are no longer economically logical or politically correct. As capital's labour market needs came to be met from increasingly diverse populations, fears arising out of concrete dangers meshed with socially constructed hatreds and bigotries, giving rise to a politics of ugliness.

Politicians claiming to be influenced by popular sentiment and/or the need to protect their population's economic welfare, always are likely to base their immigration policies and decisions on discriminatory and racist criteria. Often this will be done to off-set discontent in the electorate, a discontent that arises out of deteriorating material conditions, for which "others," rather than governments and wealth owners, are sought to be blamed.

In short, the inevitable alienation and inequality that arises out of capitalism and its immigration-based market structures deepens any existing strands of racism. But, should not a liberal democratic legal system put a stop to this tendency? Sadly much evidence in Lisa Jakubowski's work shows that it does not. It becomes clear that for a law to say "there shall be no discrimination" does not mean that there shall be no discrimination. While the law and the ideology it furthers do not permit policy-makers or law-makers to talk in explicitly racialized tones, the fact is that they may well use that very law and its ideology

8

to put racist policies into practice.

The chameleon-like nature of the law—the duplicitous ways in which the law is written, the equivocal way in which it is stated and, therefore, talked about, the hiding of the truth about the resources that are expended in its implementation, the misleading way in which it casts the discretions it purports to take away and to give—its ideological functioning and its capacity to legitimate the illegitimate, all are put under the microscope in this study. It is a timely piece of work. It may make some readers uncomfortable, but it will leave no one untouched. We are being urged to ask critical questions about everything in our polity, most of all about the way in which we hide behind a model of law and law-making that is belied by the documentation in this book that establishes the racist nature of our immigration law. We have to ask: Does our legal system hide the fact that it serves capitalism rather than liberal democracy? And, if it does, how is this done? Does the law obfuscate the fact that capitalism and democracy are antonyms? Happy Canada Day.

H.J. Glasbeek
Professor Emeritus
Osgoode Hall Law School
York University
July 1, 1996

1

Controlling Immigration:
"Race" and Canadian Immigration Law and Policy Formation

Introduction

Questions of racism in relation to Canadian immigration are complex: this book explores the process through which racism comes to be manifested in Canadian immigration law, policies and practices.

In principle, Canadian immigration law has moved from being explicitly restrictive to non-discriminatory. Prior to 1968, the overtly prejudicial law was based on a "nationality preference system" favouring European immigrants (Simmons 1990:141). However, with the emergence of the more "liberal," "non-discriminatory" points system in October of 1967, the characteristics[1] of the potential Canadian immigrant began to change. Since 1968, approximately 2.8 million immigrants from new[2] origin countries in Africa, Asia and Latin America have arrived in Canada (ibid.). This "new wave" of immigration from "Third World" countries now constitutes two-thirds of the inflow to Canada (ibid.). This chapter examines the economic, political and social implications of these legal changes.

The chapter begins with an historical overview of the literature on "race"[3] as it is manifested in Canadian immigration law, policies and practices. Throughout this review, it becomes increasingly apparent that, while the law now enables more people of colour to come to Canada, discrimination, in less obvious forms, persists. Also through this exploration, the relationship among "race," immigration, capitalism and the state begins to unfold. It becomes evident how the presence of new, visibly different immigrants expedites the persistence and advancement of capitalism in Canada.

Clearly there are links between immigration and Canadian political economy, and many theorists (e.g., Basran 1983; Bolaria and Li 1988; Cappon 1975) have attempted to analyze the relationship between state immigration policies and Canadian capitalist development. The work of Simmons, for example, highlights how Canada's immigration and refugee policies are shaped by the economic context within which they emerge.

> [T]he Canadian state has promoted immigration policies favouring relatively large inflows of immigrant workers during periods of economic expansion and more selective inflows of skilled workers, entrepreneurs and visa workers in periods of economic recession. (1992:13)

10

However, there is more to the admission of immigrants than the demands of the labour market. Historically *who* is admitted and *how many* are admitted have been determined by three, often competing factors: the desire to populate Canada with British people (or those whose characteristics most resemble the British); the need to be respecting of and attentive to concerns of the international community; and economic factors (Law Union of Ontario 1981:17). With this in mind, I examine more closely the transition, *in theory*, from discriminatory to equitable immigration legislation. Questions emerge regarding the role of the state in immigration law and policy formation. For instance, has the state, in creating non-discriminatory legislation, eradicated or exacerbated the problem of racism in Canada? For whom is the creation of a more "equitable" law most beneficial? From this initial exploration comes the conclusion that the process of law and policy formation is not as simple and straightforward as it may appear to be.

With the above overview in mind, consider first how "race," from an historical standpoint, has come to be manifested in Canadian immigration law and policy.

Nation-building and the White Canada Policy

The trends in Canadian immigration law and policy formation indicate that the content and objectives of laws and policies have been shaped by a multiplicity of factors, including ideological and political considerations, international obligations and economic requirements (Elliot and Fleras 1996:290). In the law-creation process, these factors are integrally related and law-makers recognize that, in formulating laws, competing interests must be addressed. This process becomes increasingly complex as the nation's population grows more diverse.

Since the time of Confederation, Canadian immigration laws and policies have changed considerably. However, one goal has remained constant—maintaining immigration control. Immigration can be "controlled" in blatantly discriminatory or subtle ways. Historically, in relation to Canadian immigration, the term "race" has conveniently appeared and disappeared in law. The initial appearance of the term is associated with Canada's implicit White Canada policy. Officially abandoned only in 1962, the White Canada policy was deeply rooted in the mid-nineteenth century. As Hawkins (1989:8) notes, these early origins "and indeed the whole lengthy episode of White Canada is often downplayed, or clothed in discreet silence or simply not extrapolated from its historical context."

Initially, immigration policies could be described as "racist in orientation, assimilationist in objective" (Elliot and Fleras 1996:290). Striving to preserve the British character of Canada, efforts were directed towards excluding some people from entry, while encouraging others to settle. Potential migrants were ranked into categories, with "preferred" immigrants being drawn from Great Britain, the United States, France and, to a lesser extent, Northern and Western

11

Europe (Manpower and Immigration 1974:4). When these recruitment efforts failed to produce the large numbers required to settle Canada's western prairie lands, the federal government extended its preferential policies to include other "white" immigrants—for example, Ukrainians, Italians, Poles and Hutterites— previously classified as "non-preferred" (Henry et al. 1995:72). Emphasis was placed on white immigrants because they were considered to be of "superior stock," more desirable and more assimilable than immigrants of colour (Elliot and Fleras 1996:290). However, even with the expansion of the preferred categories to include more white immigrants, Canadian labour needs could not be met. In the 1880s recruitment began of an "undesirable," visibly different source of cheap labour—the Chinese. It was during this time period that "race," in relation to Canadian immigration law and policy formation, first became an issue of significance (Henry et al. 1995:72).

One of the central events that triggered the immigration of the Chinese to Canada was the construction of the Canadian Pacific Railway (CPR). During the period of its construction (1881–85), the number of Chinese arriving in Canada rose dramatically (Bolaria and Li 1988:105). Asian immigrants were particularly attractive because of their large supply and cheap cost. While nation-building, the Chinese railway workers were tolerated by the white workers, as long as there was no other source of labour available. However when the CPR was completed, and there was a surplus of labour in Canada, sentiments towards the Asian/Chinese presence changed (ibid.). Accordingly, a conflict between business and labour arose.

It was clearly in the interests of Canadian capitalists to have a reserve army of Asian labour. According to capitalist principles, the rate at which profit is accumulated is directly related to the level of labour exploitation. To ensure that profits are maximized, labour must necessarily be induced into performing "the most undesirable tasks in production for the lowest possible costs" (Bolaria and Li 1988:28). For the capitalist, the appeal of immigrant labour, in this case Chinese labour, is precisely its willingness to do undesirable work cheaply. Aside from increasing the supply of labour and decreasing its high cost, immigrant labour "weakens the organizational efforts and bargaining position of the dominant workforce" (ibid.:34). Finally, the powerlessness of immigrants makes them extremely vulnerable to exploitation, marginalization and exclusion (Bouhdiba 1981). Particularly in times of economic crisis, they become ideal targets of blame for all of the host country's economic, social and political ills.[4] For Portes:

> the very fact of crossing a political border weakens the status of workers vis-a-vis the State. They are thus more subject to police supervision and arbitrary decisions by officials and employers. (1978:32)

Unlike the capitalists, the reaction of white Canadian labourers to the Chinese presence was less enthusiastic. The ultimate result was the emergence of a "split-labour market."

According to Bonacich, a split-labour market produces three-way conflict between the dominant class and the two groups of labourers. Initially,

> ethnic antagonism . . . germinates in a labour market split along ethnic lines. To be split, a labour market must contain at least two groups of workers whose price of labour differs for the same work, or would differ if they did the same work. (1972:549)

The dominant business class strives to maximize profits utilizing the cheapest available sources of labour power. Through the process of super-exploitation (Cox 1948), the dominant class will replace higher paid labour with cheaper labour. Bonacich (1980:15) argues that, because employers prefer to hire the cheaper labourers of colour, white workers fear and become hostile towards the more exploitable racial minorities. One way white workers can respond to this hostility and fear is to try to restrict the capitalist's access to cheaper labour through "exclusion" (Bonacich 1972:554-57, 1976:45).

In the case of exclusion, dominant white labour excludes the super-exploited workers of colour from full participation in the labour market by attempting to prevent this cheaper labour source from moving into a particular territory. The push by organized white labour to "control immigration" is one way of practising exclusion against certain visible minorities.

Returning to the case of the Chinese labourers in Canada, the above pattern becomes quite clear. Antagonistic towards and feeling threatened by these visibly different newcomers, white labourers began pressing the Canadian government to restrict immigration. The government took action, striving to address the needs of two constituencies—business and labour. When the nation-building projects such as the construction of the CPR were close to completion, the need for these cheap labourers diminished. Accordingly, the federal govern-ment began passing highly discriminatory, exclusionary pieces of immigration legislation (Henry et al. 1995:72; Elliot and Fleras 1996:290-91).

Elements of restriction, first directed towards the Chinese in 1885 and subsequently towards all immigrants of colour, began appearing in immigration legislation from the 1880s onward (Hawkins 1989:16). What must be noted here is that, while the general term "race" did not emerge as a prohibitive/restrictive "legal category" until the *Immigration Act* of 1910, specific regulations and pieces of legislation were passed by the government that were blatantly discriminatory towards certain racial minorities. In particular, the federal government decided to take action against Asian immigration and devised different methods for "discouraging immigration" from China, Japan and India (Law Union of Ontario 1981:25). Consider, by way of example, the *Chinese*

Immigration Act of 1885, the 1907 *Gentleman's Agreement* with Japan, and the *Continuous Journey Stipulation* of 1908, which was directed towards India and the curtailing of East Indian immigration.

The *Chinese Immigration Act* of 1885 imposed a head tax on all Chinese men arriving in Canada (Chinese women and children were excluded from entry into the country). While the tax was set at fifty dollars in 1885 (Statutes of Canada (SC) 1885), it rose to a hundred dollars in 1900 (SC 1900) and to five hundred dollars by 1903 (SC 1903) (Bolaria and Li 1988:107). However even with the tax, the flow of Chinese immigration continued. Facing more and more pressure to eradicate this "immigration problem," the Canadian government passed the *Chinese Exclusion Act* (SC 1923), which prohibited Chinese immigration from 1923 until the Act was repealed in 1947 (Bolaria and Li 1988:107).[5] With respect to restricting Japanese immigration, the case was a little more complicated.

The Japanese were allies of the British at the turn of the century, so if Canada were to take action against Japanese immigration, it had to do so in a way that would not jeopardize British–Japanese relations. Also, Japan had the potential to become a trading partner with Canada, so some degree of cooperation was considered "desirable" (Law Union of Ontario 1981:26). A representative of the federal government was thus sent to Japan to negotiate what came to be known as the *Gentleman's Agreement*: "Under the terms of this agreement, Canada agreed not to impose discriminatory laws against Japanese immigrants, but the Japanese government was to voluntarily restrict the number of people permitted to emigrate to Canada" (ibid.).

In the case of India, the government was not as successful in its negotiations for such an agreement. India was clearly resistant to such restrictions, and this left the Canadian government with a dilemma. Not wanting to cause rifts within the British Empire, Canada could not take direct, discriminatory action. How then could it more subtly control East Indian immigration? The solution was the *Continuous Journey Stipulation of 1908* (ibid.). According to this regulation, immigrants who came to Canada "otherwise than by continuous journey from countries of which they were natives or citizens, and upon through tickets purchased in that country, may be refused entry" (Bolaria and Li 1988:170). This particular regulation highlights the political nature of law. Because they were citizens of the British Empire, East Indians should have been entitled to immigrate to Canada, but this was made almost impossible by the *Continuous Journey Stipulation*. At that time, the only company that could provide transportation from India to Canada was the Canadian Pacific Railway. In order to achieve its exclusionary objective, the government issued the CPR express orders not to sell any "through tickets" to Canada from India (Law Union of Upper Canada 1981:26). From the standpoint of law-makers and politicians, the *Stipulation* was both functional and politically calculating.

First, the regulation did indeed curtail East Indian immigration to Canada.

For example, in 1907 and 1908 a total of 4,757 East Indians immigrated to Canada. When the *Stipulation* became effective in 1909, the numbers decreased dramatically. In 1909, only 6 East Indians were admitted to Canada, while the total admission of East Indians to Canada between 1909 and 1913 was 29 (Bolaria and Li 1988:169). Second, in an effort to preserve its positive relations with the rest of the British Empire, the Canadian government ensured that the *Stipulation* did not *explicitly* bar any particular group of people from entry into Canada. Highlighting its politicality, the *Continuous Journey Stipulation* "amended the *Immigration Act* to allow the government to control East Indian immigration without having the appearance of doing so" (Henry et al. 1995:73).

The now famous "Komagata Maru Incident" was an attempt by East Indians to challenge this racist policy. On May 23, 1914 a ship called *Komagata Maru* arrived in Vancouver carrying 376, mostly Sikh, passengers. Because the ship had made numerous stops along the way to pick up people, the passengers were denied entry into Canada under the *Continuous Journey Stipulation*. After a two-month standoff between East Indians and the Canadian government, the *Komagata Maru* was escorted out of Vancouver harbour by a navel ship. The efforts of the East Indians failed during the summer months of 1914 but, to this day, various East Indian organizations continue to demand compensation and an admission, by the federal government, of wrongdoing in the incident of *Komagata Maru* (Elliot and Fleras 1992:240; Bolaria and Li 1988:171).

In essence, the *Chinese Exclusion Act*, the *Gentleman's Agreement* and the *Continuous Journey Stipulation* were effective mechanisms for controlling immigration, ensuring that almost no Asians emigrated to Canada until after the Second World War (Henry et al. 1995:73). Such mechanisms were consistent with the philosophy towards immigration that had emerged in the late nineteenth and early twentieth centuries. A quotation from an immigration promotional pamphlet of the time, entitled *Canada—The New Homeland,* makes this philosophy crystal clear:

> Canada is situated in the North Temperate Zone. . . . The climate is particularly suited to the white race. It is the land of homes—the new homeland of the British people. . . . British people soon find themselves at home in Canada. It is a British country, with British customs and ideals. . . . (as cited in Law Union of Ontario 1981:26)

The Advent of "Race" in Canadian Immigration Law

The term "race" first emerged as a prohibitive/restrictive legal category in Section 38(c) of the *Immigration Act* of 1910 (Hawkins 1989:17). This Section, amended in 1919 to include "nationality," is most representative of White Canada's xenophobia. In essence, Section 38(c) created a class of immigrants considered to be "undesirable" for admission to Canada. Included among those who could be denied entry were:

> any *nationality* or *race* of immigrants of any specified class or occupation, by reason of any economic, industrial or other condition temporarily existing in Canada or because such immigrants are *deemed unsuitable* having regard to the climatic, industrial, social, educational, labour . . . or because such immigrants are deemed *undesirable* owing to their peculiar customs, habits, modes of life, methods of holding property and because of their probable inability to become readily assimilated or to assume the duties and responsibilities of Canadian citizenship within a reasonable time after their entry. (emphasis added)

By including Section 38(c) in the *Immigration Act,* the government's discriminatory policies were enshrined in law—differential treatment based on "race" or nationality was firmly established as a government policy. One form of differential treatment was the creation of a list of "preferred" countries:

> The policy of the Department at the present time [1910] is to encourage immigration of farmers, farm labourers, and female domestic servants from the United States, the British Isles, and certain Northern European countries, namely, France, Belgium, Holland, Switzerland, Germany, Denmark, Norway, Sweden and Iceland. On the other hand, it is the policy of the Department *to do all in its power to keep out of the country . . . those belonging to nationalities unlikely to assimilate and who consequently prevent the building up of a united nation of people of similar customs and ideals.* (Manpower and Immigration 1974: 9-10, emphasis added)

Most conveniently, the legislation of 1910 did not specify the "undesirable" countries. Instead, it gave immigration officials "wide discretion to exclude almost any prospective immigrant on the basis of race, national or ethnic origin or creed" (Henry et al. 1995:73).

From the outbreak of the First World War, through the Depression and the Second World War, Canadian immigration went through a long period of uncertainty (Manpower and Immigration 1974:10). In response to the need to settle Western Canada, immigration had peaked at 400,870 in 1913. However, the unstable and uncertain conditions generated by the two world wars and the Depression resulted in fewer people coming to Canada, with immigration reaching an all-time low of 7,576 in 1942 (Elliot and Fleras 1996:291). Following the Second World War, immigration rates once again skyrocketed in response to a post-war boom in the Canadian economy. But even with an overwhelming need for labour, "discrimination and ethnic selectivity in immigration would remain" (Reimers and Troper 1992:20).

The "peacetime policy" (Manpower and Immigration 1974:18) was unveiled in Prime Minister Mackenzie King's 1947 *Statement on Immigration*:

> With regard to the selection of immigrants. . . . I wish to make it quite clear that Canada is perfectly within her rights in selecting persons who we regard as desirable future citizens. It is not a "fundamental human right" of any alien to enter Canada. It is a privilege. It is a matter of domestic policy. . . . [T]he people of Canada do not wish, as a result of mass immigration, to make a fundamental alteration in the character of our population. Large scale immigration from the Orient would change the fundamental character of the Canadian population. . . . [T]he government therefore . . . has no intention of removing existing regulations respecting Asiatic immigration unless and until alternative measures of effective control have been worked out. (Manpower and Immigration 1974:205)

Essentially, this excerpt highlights how with the rejuvenation of immigration in 1947 came a return to the "policy, regulations and racial priorities of an earlier era" (Reimers and Troper 1992:21)—that is, policies were still racist in orientation, assimilationist in objective. Care would still be taken to ensure that those applicants from groups considered to be "most easily assimilated," i.e., "British subjects from the United Kingdom, Ireland, Newfoundland, New Zealand, Australia or the Union of South Africa, and also citizens of the United States" (King, in Manpower and Immigration 1974:203), would be given preferential treatment during the admission process. To reinforce this xenophobic position, the *Immigration Act* of 1952 maintained the explicitly restrictive clause 38(c), although the category "race" was changed to "ethnic group" (Hawkins 1989:17). Consistent with the exclusions that had been outlined in the 1910 *Act*, the minister was given wide-sweeping discretion to prohibit or limit the admission of people on the basis of ethnicity, nationality, geographic origin, peculiarity of custom, unsuitability of climate or inability to become assimilated (Reimers and Troper 1992:25). Through the use of such discretion, the "national and racial balance of immigration would be regulated so as to not to disturb the existing "character" of the Canadian population (Green 1976:21).

Abandoning the White Canada Policy
—Fact or Fiction?

From the *Immigration Act* of 1910 up to and including the *Act* of 1952, Section 38(c) was the principal instrument through which the implicit White Canada policy in immigration was implemented. However with the passage of new, non-discriminatory Immigration Regulations in 1962, the White Canada policy was, as Hawkins (1989:39) notes, "virtually dead." These regulations officially ended racial and ethnic discrimination in the processing of independent immigrants, with "skills," or more specifically, "skills in relation to Canadian labour market needs," becoming the main selection criterion (Reimers and Troper 1992:32). This shift towards universal and equal treatment of all applicants was reinforced in the White Paper of 1966,[6] which proposed that all persons coming to Canada as immigrants would be subject to the same entrance standards, regardless of "race," religion or country of origin.

It is important to note that these policy changes towards non-discriminatory treatment were not necessarily made in response to popular demand in Canada. In fact, Hawkins suggests that change occurred because senior Canadian officials realized that "Canada could not operate effectively with the United Nations, or in a multiracial Commonwealth, with the millstone of a racially discriminatory immigration policy round her neck" (1989:39). But if "race," nationality, and ethnicity could no longer be used explicitly as a rationale for selecting immigrants, some other system had to be created that could be applied in a way that was "reasonably fair and objective" (ibid.). Accordingly, in October of 1967, Canada developed the first immigration "points system."

The purpose of the points system was to establish an "objective" assessment system for the admission of immigrants. The criteria for admission were: education and training; personal assessment; occupational demand; occupational skill; age; arranged employment; knowledge of French or English; relatives; and employment opportunities in area of destination (Hawkins 1988:405). The nine factors have a combined potential value of one hundred. If an applicant received fifty or more points, s/he was considered likely to settle successfully. If the applicant received less than fifty points, success at settlement was deemed unlikely[7] (Manpower and Immigration 1974:42). While the original points system was revised in 1974, 1978 and 1985 (Hawkins 1988:380), its intent remained the same—that is, immigration policy would be applied on "a universal basis which can be interpreted to mean that everyone seeking admission to Canada is assessed under the same set of standards regardless of race, religion or country of origin" (Green 1976:42).

Although the establishment of "a formally colour-blind immigration policy" (Elliot and Fleras 1996:292) made it appear as though racial discrimination had been eliminated, there was evidence to the contrary (ibid; Henry et al. 1995; Bolaria and Li 1988; Malarek 1987; Green 1976). There were no longer blatantly discriminatory provisions within the regulations, but subtle discriminatory mechanisms remain. As an example, consider the issue of immigration offices outside of Canada. Green notes that:

> as the government shifts from a national/ethnic-based policy to a universal admission approach, it would have to expand its overseas offices so that, in theory at least, right of review was equal for prospective immigrants regardless of their country of origin. (1976:43)

However, as Green's analysis of overseas expenditures indicates, from 1951 to 1969, the largest concentration of resources committed to the recruitment of migrants was in "developed," traditional source countries (47–54). Specifically, between 1951 and 1957, 91.39 percent of total expenditures for recruitment went to developed countries, compared to 8.61 percent to less developed countries. Between 1962 and 1969, the distribution of resources still remained largely unbalanced, with 78.2 percent of total expenditures for recruitment going to developed countries, compared to 21.8 percent for less developed countries (47). As Anthony Richmond observed: "there [was] evidently no intention of abandoning the traditional preference for British immigrants" (in Green 1976:51).

The commitment, in theory, to the elimination of racial discrimination was more formally enshrined in the *Immigration Act* of 1976. Consistent with trends of past immigration law and policy formation, the decision to include a non-discriminatory clause in the *Act* was shaped by the interplay among several factors. From an economic standpoint, Canada moved from "a dependence on unskilled manual labour toward a more highly educated and skilled workforce" (Henry et al. 1995:76). Because of a decline in immigration from traditional source countries (due to post-war economic recovery), Canada opened its doors to "non-preferred" countries in search of economically suitable immigrants. From a more political and social standpoint, pressure to eradicate overt racism surfaced. Influences ranged from a newly implemented multicultural policy that recognized racial and cultural diversity in Canada to increasing pressure from well-organized, politically active and increasingly influential minority groups, human rights activists and lawyers and the international community (ibid.). In response to the various influences, Section 3(f) emerged:

> It is hereby declared that Canadian Immigration policy and the rules and regulations made under this *Act* shall be designed and administered in such a manner as to promote the domestic and international interests of Canada recognizing the need to . . . (f) *ensure that any person who seeks admission to Canada on either a permanent or temporary basis is subject to standards of admission that do not discriminate on grounds of race, national or ethnic origin, colour, religion or sex.* (Hawkins 1988:426, emphasis added)

Under the *Act*, all immigrants would be assessed according to "universal standards" designed to assess ability to "adapt to Canadian life" and settle successfully. The passage of this *Act* into law in 1978 was hailed by some as an extremely positive and important moment in Canadian history. For instance, in the words of Freda Hawkins (1988:xv): "this marked the beginning of a new, more liberal and more cooperative era in Canadian immigration." But, were these legislative changes in practice as positive as they appeared to be on paper?

Despite the more universal system and the commitment *in theory* to equality, discrimination in less obvious forms persisted.

For instance, even with the 1976 *Act*, a discriminatory policy can be seen in the distribution of immigration offices. By way of example:

> there are five immigration offices in the United Kingdom, but only three in South America, and only five in the whole of Africa, two of which are located in South Africa. The United States has ten offices, but India, with twice the population only has one. (Law Union of Ontario 1981:46)

Following the passage of the *Act*, this distribution of immigration offices clearly indicated the "historical preference for white European immigration" (ibid.). Furthermore, the wide use of discretion under the *Act* and regulations allows individual, biased officers to make discriminatory decisions (ibid.).

Under the original points system, "personal assessment" was the only criterion that involved a subjective judgement on the part of the immigration officer (Manpower and Immigration 1974:44). This factor was worth fifteen points out of one hundred. Immigration officers were to use their discretion in deciding on "a person's ability to become settled in a new country", based on the officer's perceptions of the applicant's adaptability, motivation, initiation and resourcefulness (ibid.). This criterion still exists within the points system, but is now worth ten points and is called "personal suitability" (Young 1991a:20).

The weighting of the personal suitability criterion implies some limitation on the immigration officer's discretion. However, the officer's discretion extends well beyond this criterion. A regulation was introduced that grants officers the discretion to override the points system "in exceptional cases." The justification for the inclusion of this regulation is clearly outlined in the following statement by Manpower and Immigration:

> Introduction of weighted selection factors in 1967 was a totally new immigration concept. It was hoped that totalling the units of assessment awarded for each of the factors would indicate, within reasonable limits, the likelihood of most applicants' success or failure in becoming established in Canada. It was recognized however, that it was impossible to cover every eventuality, and that the regulations should contain a mechanism for dealing with the exceptional case. Accordingly, when a selection officer is satisfied that there are significant circumstances affecting an applicant's prospects that have not been reflected in the assessment under the nine selection factors he [sic] is authorized, subject to concurrence of a designated senior officer, to accept or reject the applicant *irrespective of the number of units of assessment that may have been awarded.* (1974:50, emphasis added)

This discretion continues to the present day. Section 11(3) of the Immigration Regulations

> authorizes officers to exercise their discretion in respect of immigrants whose applications are unit-rated under the selection criteria, and to accept, or refuse to accept an applicant, whether the applicant achieves or does not achieve the number of units of assessment. Discretion . . . is . . . exercised . . . solely on the basis that the unit-rating does not accurately reflect an immigrant's chances of becoming successfully established in Canada. (Employment and Immigration Canada 1991:07-90-6)

Conclusion

What conclusions can be drawn from the above discussion? *In principle*, Canadian immigration law has moved from being explicitly restrictive to non-discriminatory. The explicitly restrictive clause (Section 38(c)) of the 1910, 1919 and 1952 *Acts* has been removed. In fact, since 1962 there has been a shift towards universal, non-discriminatory treatment of all applicants applying for admission to Canada. The principle of equality is now embodied in Section 3(f) of Canada's *Immigration Act*.

While acknowledging these literal gains, the non-discriminatory *Immigration Act* is not as just and fair as it appears to be. The language of discrimination may have been removed but, in less obvious ways, immigration law is still racist. The number and location of immigration offices outside of Canada and the discretion awarded to immigration officers in determining adaptability suggests that immigration, to some degree, is still being "controlled."

This preliminary review intimates that one must problematize, rather than unquestioningly accept, the claim that Canada's immigration law is non-discriminatory. Although couched in the politically acceptable language of equity and fairness, does this automatically mean that the law is equitably applied to all potential immigrants at the point of entry? In this book, I will substantively explore how racism is manifested in contemporary Canadian immigration law and policies. Specifically, I will analyze federal government documents and their accounts of two amendments to Canada's *Immigration Act*: the *Live-In Caregiver Program* and Bill C-86. Throughout, I will emphasize how these legislative changes reinforce already-existing forms of systemic discrimination and "naturalize"[8] social inequality among the "races."

In order to better appreciate the complexities underlying the process of Canadian immigration law and policy formation, some contextualization is necessary. With this in mind, I now turn to a theoretical review of various dimensions of the sociology of law as they are relevant to my forthcoming analysis of contemporary Canadian immigration law.

Notes

1. For the purposes of clarification, the government includes the following groups within the category "visible minority": Blacks, Chinese, Japanese, Koreans, Filipinos, Indo-Pakistanis, West Asians and Arabs, Southeast Asians, Latin Americans and Pacific Islanders (Elliot and Fleras 1992:249).

2. According to de Silva (1992:3-4), immigrants are classified as either "traditional" or "new" on the basis of their country of origin and skin colour. Although classification on the basis of these criteria is far from perfect, it appears that, for the most part, "traditional" immigrants are white whereas "new" immigrants are visibly different.

3. Throughout this book the term "race" will be used in quotation marks in formal acknowledgement of its uselessness as an analytic term (Miles 1989:72; Guillaumin 1980:39). "Race" is an ideological construction that has "profound meanings in the everyday world, but which has no scientific credibility" (Miles 1984:232). I do not want to further reinforce the commonsensical understanding of this term. Instead, I wish to highlight that awarding analytical power to the word "race," or using it uncritically, lends legitimacy to the misconception that "races" are real or correctly apprehensible. For a more detailed discussion of why the concept of "race" has been scientifically discredited, the reader is referred to Rex (1983).

4. When it is in the interests of the powerful to do so, "villainizing" the immigrant becomes a common practice. A case in point is the introduction of Bill C-86 by the Conservative government in June 1992. For more on Bill C-86, see Chapter Five.

5. Although the *Chinese Exclusion Act* was repealed in 1947 after the Second World War, the only category of immigration open to the Chinese, until 1962, was "sponsored relatives" of Chinese Canadians (Bolaria and Li 1988:118).

6. This paper initially emerged in response to the post-war, unlimited sponsorship movement. The movement produced a largely unskilled workforce, incompatible with Canada's economic needs. This coupled with increasing unemployment was, in the eyes of the government, cause for concern. Lack of immigration control could only exacerbate the problem. For a more detailed discussion see Hawkins (1988:50ff).

7. Under the current points system, an independent immigrant must receive seventy points before being considered to "have the potential to adapt successfully to Canada and be of benefit to this country socially and economically" (Young 1991a:18).

8. In this context, the term "naturalize" is used in a particular way. Specifically, when something is "naturalized," it becomes unquestioned, taken for granted or perceived to be just common sense.

2

The Question of Social Order:
Exploring the Duality of Law

Introduction

The doctrine of the "Rule of Law" states

> that political power should be exercised according to rules announced in advance. A political system is analogous to a game—it is only fair to give prior notice of the rules to all the participants and then to insist that everyone abide by them, even in adversity. The rule of law does not require that laws should have a particular kind of content, but *simply that they should constrain the weak and the powerful alike*. Such a principle inhibits arbitrary despots and authoritarian oligarchies from dispossessing citizens of their liberties without cause shown. (Collins 1982:12, emphasis added)

In principle, the Rule of Law imposes effective inhibitions on power and this is "an unqualified human good" (Thompson 1982:135). It represents an ideal to which various applications of the law might be compared. In its ideal form, law inspires social change and has the potential to drastically reduce or eliminate inequality among human beings (Sumner 1982:260). However, the essence of the Rule of Law is lost when this principle is appropriated and used to perpetuate and normalize unequal social relations within a social formation.

This chapter explores the role of law in reconstituting and legitimizing unequal social relations. Conceptualizing law as ideology, the legal treatment of "difference" in relation to the reproduction, "naturalization" and legitimation of privilege is examined. More specifically, in the social construction of law, accounts of social reality are created that appear to be detached from particular subjectivities. Stemming from this appearance of detachment, law purports to be an objective and neutral form of knowledge. Objectivity and neutrality however, are often little more than appearances. As with other forms of human activity, law is an ideological discourse that is shaped by and reflective of the interests and experiences of those who participate in a society's defining structures. This shall be illustrated by emphasizing the duality of law in relation to the exercise of various forms of power—economic, male-supremacist and racist. Before considering law's specific role in reflecting dominant economic and social interests, some contextualization is in order. I begin, therefore, with a more general review of ideology as it is related to law and the process of hegemony.

Ideology: The Foundations of a Conceptual Framework

Initially defined as "doctrines of ideas" (McLellan 1986:6), ideologies can be utilized to maintain social order or promote social change (Allahar 1986:616). Central to the present analysis is some consideration of the way(s) in which ideology assists in the reproduction, legitimation and naturalization of privilege on the basis of difference. Such a discussion benefits from a review of the nature of ideology and the classical contributions of Marx, Engels and Weber.

The contributions of Marx and Engels

The work of Marx and Engels highlights how "systems of ideas" can be both illusory or distorting and socially regulating.[1] By highlighting its illusory and regulatory quality in relation to class, Marx and Engels allude to the usefulness of ideology for creating illusions about the nature of capitalism.

> The ideas of the ruling class are in every epoch the ruling ideas, i.e., *the class which is the ruling material force of society, is at the same time its ruling intellectual force*. The class which has the means of material production at its disposal, has control at the same time over the means of mental production, so that thereby, generally speaking, the ideas of those who lack the means of mental production are subject to it. *The ruling ideas are nothing more than* the ideal expression of the dominant material relationships, *the dominant material relationships expressed as ideas*; hence of the relationships which make the one class the ruling one, therefore, the ideas of its dominance. (1986:64, emphasis added)

Because the ruling class enjoys a "monopoly" over the means of both material and mental production, it will regulate the production and distribution of ideas in a way that is consistent with protecting its interests in the field of material production. These ideologies, then,

> set limits to the consciousness of the ruled classes. . . . To maintain social order and stability . . . those with a direct stake in maintaining the status quo convince the less privileged that the system works to the mutual benefit of everyone in it. . . . (Allahar 1986:617)

In this context, ideologies serve to "justify and legitimize the rule of the few over the many" (Allahar 1989:14).

The work of Marx and Engels sensitizes the reader to the ways in which ideology can be used to create the illusion of a capitalist society as "just." By maintaining such an image, the legitimacy of those in positions of power can be preserved. Ideologies, however, are not exclusively related to domination and class interests. From a psychological standpoint, ideologies help individuals "to impose some sense of order and direction upon the social world" (Miles and Phizacklea 1984:7). Interestingly, this more subjective, psychological feature was also explicit in the writings of Weber (Birnbaum 1953:131-32).

The contributions of Weber

Weber (1968) contends that an understanding of ideology could not be complete without a consideration of the fundamental, non-economic factors that affect human action. Preoccupied with showing how "ideas become effective forces in history" (1958:90), Weber provides evidence to suggest that human behaviour is influenced as much by one's state of mind as it is by material interests. This evidence emerges from an examination of how religious beliefs, the Protestant Ethic in particular, affected the development and emergence of modern capitalist society (ibid.).

A central theme in Weber's argument is that the behaviour generated by Protestant beliefs was related to the individual's need to maintain some sense of mental stability in the face of salvation anxiety. Any subsequent impact that this behaviour may have had on economic development was unanticipated. Consider, for example, the Calvinist doctrine of predestination. There was a tremendous strain associated with not knowing whether one was chosen for salvation. Thus, people had to consider themselves "elected" and combat all sense of doubt through strict self-denial and hard work (Zeitlin 1987:117). This behaviour, which was a response to the beliefs and teachings of Calvinism, coincidentally generated much of the cultural foundation of early capitalism: "individualism, achievement motivation, opposition to magic and superstition, and a commitment to organization and calculation in personal and public life" (Abercrombie et al. 1988:198).

It is in relation to ideology that Weber's work is particularly significant. His study highlights the importance of beliefs rather than ideas. Accordingly, ideology can be conceptualized "primarily as a system of beliefs and only secondarily of ideas" (Rejai 1971:3). Rejai defined belief systems as

> interrelated sets of notions and attitudes about man [sic] and society, that are accepted, at least in part, as a matter of habitual reinforcement and routinization. Beliefs, in short, say nothing about the truthfulness or falsity of a notion or an attitude; they imply only a psychological state of acceptance. (ibid.)

Ideas and beliefs differ in the sense that "ideas are subject to scientific operation (such as testing and verification), whereas beliefs are not" (ibid.).

The introduction of a belief/idea dichotomy enhances the usefulness of Weber's (1958) analysis of the effects of religion on human behaviour. While he discusses religious beliefs in particular, the concept of belief can be utilized to address different questions. It can, for example, be applied to a consideration of inquiries regarding issues of legitimacy and authority. Specifically, one can examine the way(s) in which various institutions promote widespread and largely unquestioned acceptance of the justness of the unequal social order by practising processes of "habitual reinforcement" and "routinization." These reinforcement processes, however, are complicated by the personalized and subjective nature of belief systems.

In helping individuals to make sense of and develop stability within their social worlds, ideologies represent individualized forms of adaptation. The way one adapts in society may not be consistent with the dominant interest to naturalize a particular conception of the social order. As Miles and Phizacklea (1984:9) note,

> people can test ideas and interpretations they receive . . . against their own experience of the world. Ideology [therefore] is not only "handed down." It is constantly being created and renewed by people in response to the world as they experience it.

The way one *responds*, in this case to the ideological notion of society as good or just, is ideology's "programmatic" dimension. The response, whether supportive or critical, represents "a call for action that translates specific values, norms and ideas into practice. Such actions are aimed at either maintaining the status quo or transforming it" (Allahar 1989:17). In this sense, ideology is central to hegemony.

Ideology and its Relationship to Hegemony

Hegemony is the term used by Gramsci (1971) to describe the process by which one group, using both physically coercive and ideological means, achieves domination over others. An appreciation of the hegemonic process requires a consideration of the fundamental notions of struggle and "popular consent" (Hall 1988:53).

Before a group can become dominant, it must achieve positions of leadership simultaneously in a number of different sites of social life (ibid.). Success depends upon the willingness of various advantaged factions to construct alliances between different sectors and social forces. Also essential to this construction process is the ability of the allied force to win popular consent for its authority among the dominated classes (ibid.). Given the inherent intricacy of society, however, the establishment and maintenance of a position of superiority is not easily achieved.

According to Mouffe (1988:90) society is a "complex ensemble of heterogeneous social relations possessing their own dynamism." Relations include, but are not reducible to, the social relations of production (ibid.). Whether based on "race," gender or class, all social relations are constructed as "relations of subordination" and are potential sites of antagonism, conflict and struggle. Consequently, there are many fronts upon which resistance to subordination and inequality may occur (ibid.:91), making far more complex the process by which one group establishes domination over another. Fundamental to the struggle that constructs or transforms hegemony is ideology or, more specifically, its "common sense" component.

Common sense is something which is "close to the people" (Gramsci 1971:396). It is historically specific and represents "the traditional popular conception of the world—what is unimaginatively called 'instinct'" (ibid.:199). Common sense is "a conception formed in the closest relation to practical, everyday life" (Hall et al. 1978:154). Generally, it refers to the "uncritical and largely unconscious way of perceiving and understanding the world that has become common in any given epoch" (Gramsci 1971:323). As Nowell-Smith explains,

> [t]he key to common sense is that the ideas it embodies are not so much incorrect as uncorrected and taken for granted. . . . Common sense consists of all those ideas which can be tagged onto existing knowledge without challenging it. It offers no criteria for determining how things are in capitalist society but only a criterion of how things fit with the ways of looking at the world that the present phase of class society has inherited from the preceding one. (in Hall et al. 1978:154)

This excerpt generates two particularly salient ideas. First, common sense is related to that which is taken for granted. Second, it is made up of those ideas that filter into the existing sphere of knowledge without posing a threat to it. Utilizing Rejai's (1971) belief/idea dichotomy, common sense becomes central for the transformation of ideas into beliefs. This process is also facilitated by "complementarity."

According to Baldus (1977:250), complementary conditions are those "already-existing conditions" in society that further dominant interests. Where complementarity is present, existing social conditions and the behaviours of individuals within those conditions coalesce in a way that complements the interests of the status quo (Baldus 1975, 1977).

At this point it must be emphasized that the association between ideology and complementarity is highlighted to illustrate *one* way that those in power might reconstitute their positions of superiority. This particular focus should in no way be construed as an attempt to undermine the subjectivity and agency of individuals belonging to the dominated classes or their potential to resist the dominant ideas. The illustration to follow simply alludes to one of many ways individuals may interpret and respond to ideas.

Having made the above acknowledgement, how, in a Canadian context, can dominant interests be reconstructed and legitimized most effectively? Ideologically, a position of superiority will be most secure if individuals unquestioningly accept social inequalities as normal or natural elements of social life. The complementarity concept allows for the examination of the way in which already-existing conditions within particular societal institutions simultaneously further the interests of the powerful *and* promote the image of a just Canada. To explain this, the notion of complementarity is useful:

> periphery units are often not aware of the complementarity of their own behaviour. Moreover, the use of complementary periphery behaviour does not require an interaction between dominant class and periphery. ... The use of complementary behaviour therefore allows the dominant class to obtain needed means from a periphery which appears to pursue goals of its own choice, and free of outside interference (ibid.:251).

Through complementarity, individuals in the periphery believe that they are independently pursuing their own interests, free of dominant interference. Consequently, the legitimacy of those holding positions of authority is unlikely to be threatened.

Thus, the presence of complementary conditions can effectively convert ideas into beliefs. The transformation from ideas to beliefs emerges from within already-existing social conditions and is consistent with the behaviour of individuals acting within those conditions. More generally, this process of conversion from ideas into beliefs occurs most easily when an unquestioned acceptance of the naturalness of the unequal social order emerges among the dominated groups.

The construction or transformation of hegemony involves popular consent in the realm of civil society. "Winning over the masses" often involves winning ideological struggles on many fronts, including law, the family, the church, unions and schools. This analysis proceeds with an examination of the way in which common sense ideology is utilized in a particular site of civil society—law. Law and its institutions, as transmitters of attitudes towards justice, advance a distorted perception of justice wherein social inequality, or the privileging of some over others on the basis of difference, is naturalized. In doing so, law encourages the unjust treatment of society's less advantaged to remain unquestioned. In relation to law and policy formation, how is popular consent achieved in the realm of civil society? And what is the role of the state in this phase of the hegemonic process?

The Role of Law in the Capitalist, Liberal-Democratic State

It is interesting that, even though one of the cornerstones of capitalism is inequality, prevailing common sense maintains that we live in a just country where all Canadians share certain basic rights like liberty and equality. Canadians are likely to believe in the "justness" of Canada because clear statements to this effect have been codified in law. For example, Section 15(1) of the Canadian *Charter of Rights and Freedoms* explicitly states that

> [e]very individual is equal before and under the law, and has the right to equal protection and equal benefit of the law without discrimination and, in particular, without discrimination based on race, national or ethnic origin, colour, religion, sex, age or mental or physical disability. (in Kallen 1989:232)

If inequality is one of the defining features of Canadian society, how is the image of Canada as a just nation sustained? How, in other words, does one reconcile the contradiction between the ideology and practice of equality? It is this process of reconciliation that represents the fundamental challenge facing Canada's liberal-democratic state.

In essence, the problem for the Canadian state becomes how to fulfil its two, often contradictory functions: accumulation and legitimation (O'Connor 1973:6; Panitch 1977:8). According to O'Connor:

> the capitalistic state must try to fulfil two basic and often mutually contradictory functions—accumulation and legitimation. . . . This means that the state must try to maintain or create the conditions in which profitable capital accumulation is possible. However, the state must also try and maintain or create the conditions for social harmony. *A capitalist state that openly uses its coercive forces to help one class accumulate capital at the expense of other classes loses its legitimacy and hence undermines the basis of loyalty and support.* (1973:6, emphasis added)

This quotation suggests that the ultimate source of social stability within capitalist, liberal democracies is the legitimacy of the system. Maintaining that the basis of legitimacy within modern society is the law, I now turn to a consideration of how law contributes to the ordering of social life (Silbey 1989:1).

Law and the Question of Social Order
Law as "transcendent"

One of the original and fundamental questions to emerge among sociologists of law was: What is the relationship between law and social order? The nature of this relationship has traditionally been debated within the conflict and consensus paradigms (Burtch 1992:2; Hopkins 1975:610). From a consensus perspective, law is depicted as a product of value–consensus, an expression of "those societal values which transcends the immediate interests of individuals or groups" (Chambliss 1969:8; see, for example, Durkheim 1964b; Friedmann 1959; Bohannan 1973; Sawer 1965). As an institutionalized set of norms defining the limits of legitimate action (Parsons 1951:118), law is considered to be essential for the establishment and maintenance of social order. Within the conflict tradition on the other hand, law is generally understood to be an expression or reflection of the interests of the powerful. One of the most obvious examples here comes from Marx and Engels (see, for example, Marx 1964:223, 225-27), who identified law as a social institution created by the ruling class to further its own interests. Although these positions appear to be oppositional, one can draw parallels between the consensus and conflict orientations. For instance, within each of these frameworks, law is portrayed as a phenomenon which exists independently of the individuals who construct and/or transform it. Furthermore, each position alludes to the centrality of law in reinforcing relations of ruling. Consider first the consensus or "functionalist" paradigm.

Arguably, Emile Durkheim provides one of the most enduring functionalist analyses of law. Durkheim was fundamentally preoccupied with questions of social order, and one might best characterize his interest in law as "tangential or indirect . . . .[L]aw [is] a prime example of the concretisation or objectification of social norms and values" (Hunt 1982:30-31). Durkheim maintained that law, as a functionally integrative mechanism, was key to social solidarity. Specifically, "social cohesion rises from the collective sentiments, attitudes and values which are products of social forces that operate upon individuals. Social cohesion is thus rooted in the normative system of society" (ibid.:42-43).

What persists in Durkheim's analysis is the notion that law, in any given culture, is intimately linked to "the general form of its social structure and the division of labour" (Beirne and Quinney 1982:23). For example, in relatively simple societies, social order and cohesiveness are products of a strong "collective conscience"—that is, the number of ideas and beliefs common to the group is greater than the ideas, beliefs and tendencies unique to each individual. In more complex societies, the strength of the collective conscience decreases, being replaced by a more diversified system of ideas and beliefs representative of increased differentiation within the labour force. Thus, in the transition from simple to complex societies, the function of law changes from one that enforces a common morality to one that coordinates the activities of a diversified, differentiated society (Durkheim 1964b:70-132; Hunt 1982:37).

According to Durkheim, laws exist independently of individuals and exercise coercive power over individuals. For Durkheim (1964a:3) then, laws are "social facts": "ways of acting, thinking and feeling, external to the individual, and endowed with a power of coercion, by reason of which they control him [sic]." Consistent with the anti-individualism within his work, Durkheim focuses on the collective aspects of social facts. For example, society, as a social fact, is "not a mere sum of individuals. Rather the system formed by their association represents a specific reality which has its own characteristics"

(Durkheim 1964b:103). If society exists independently of the individuals who constitute it, then so too do the society's ideas and values (Hunt 1982:29). Thus society, its ideas and values (collective conscience) are realities *sui generis*— in and of themselves.

Law, as an expression of societal values that transcends individuals, is a reality *sui generis*. Understood in this way, law becomes one mechanism through which the existing social order can be maintained. Specifically, law is conceptualized as a functionally integrative mechanism. By emphasizing the positive (e.g., integrative) rather than the negative (e.g., coercive and constraining) dimensions of law, Durkheim provides for us the conceptual means to better understand the mobilization of popular support, among the masses, for those in positions of power and dominance.

Law is described as an instrument of the state to be used, along with other institutions, to "create and maintain a certain type of civilization and citizen" (Gramsci 1971:246). Admittedly, "law necessarily punishes" (ibid.), but all in the interests of the higher good of civilizing society. Appealing to a higher good in this way has a very important implication. Law, by appearing to transcend boundaries of class, "race" and gender, can be used to distract attention away from a problematic situation in order to unite a potentially divided population. In this case, the common ideal is "civilizing society." An appeal is made to members of a community to overlook their differences and unite in the interests of the greater good of civilizing society. The implication of joining together as a unified homogeneous group is that differences that are a function of "race," gender and class are, at least temporarily, overlooked. When the notion of a community "linked into an organic unity" (Hall 1988:62) is successfully constructed, individuals believe that "what [they] share as a nation is larger and more inclusive than what divides them into [class, "race" or gender categories]" (ibid.; see also Hunt 1991:116-17, 120).

Thus, as an ideological process, law is central to hegemony. Law is constructed and equated with reason, associated with civilization, peace and security, and characterized as the "embodiment of the bond between citizen and nation" (Hunt 1991:116-17). Accordingly, law occupies an increasingly significant role in the process through which social orders are legitimated.[2] Stemming from this reformulation/extension of the functionalist paradigm in relation to law, one can draw parallels between the works of Durkheim and Marx and Engels.

From a traditional Marxist perspective, law primarily acts as an ideological mechanism (Beirne and Quinney 1982:24; Cain 1982:68). As part of society's superstructure, law is determined by the needs of "an infrastructure of productive forces and productive relations" (Thompson 1982:132). Beginning with the premise that in the last instance economic relations have primacy, instrumentalists have argued that law is a tool of the ruling class that can be manipulated at will. Hence, the Rule of Law is nothing more than another mask for "the rule of a class" (Thompson 1982:131). Functioning coercively to back up the rules of those in positions of dominance (Collins 1982:30), law is a form of power (Turk 1976:279-80).

In a general sense, Marxism challenges the liberal contention that law can be objective and neutral. Building upon this premise, a number of themes emerge within the Marxist tradition regarding the nature of law[3]: (1) law is political; (2) law and the state are interconnected, although law exhibits a relative autonomy from the state; (3) law is expressive of the prevailing economic relations; (4) law is always potentially coercive or repressive; (5) the content of law directly or indirectly reflects the interests of the dominant class or those in positions of power; and (6) law is ideological—"it exemplifies and provides legitimation for the values of the dominant class" (Hunt 1991:102-03).

In this brief exploration of the relationship between law and social order, I have discussed law as both a functionally integrative and coercive mechanism. Because both the value–consensus and conflict traditions provide macro/ structural interpretations of the law, they have been criticized for insufficient consideration of the role of individuals in constructing, perpetuating and/or changing the law. Law is depicted as something that is external to, stands apart from, or exists independently of individuals. Whether stressing the positive (integrative) or negative (coercive) dimensions, these more traditional conceptualizations stress the power that law has over the individual. There is, however, a strain of thought emerging from within the writings of Marx that very much highlights the agency of individuals in the law creation process.

Creating Laws: The Role of the Subject

The tendency to associate Marxist interpretations of the law with structure rather than agency stems from early economistic interpretations of the Marxist theory of historical materialism within which law, as an element of the superstructure, was portrayed as nothing more than a direct reflection of the base (Collins 1982:23). Law, however, is not simply a *reflection* of the base. It is *created* by individuals who are active participants in the relations of ruling. An appreciation of the role of the individual in linking the material base to the legal superstructure is facilitated by the concept of social class (ibid.:30).

For Marx, social class is based strictly on one's position in the relations of production. And it is this position, and the practical experiences by which it is accompanied, that provide the foundation for various forms of social class "consciousness." Ideas and knowledge about the world are constructed in response to one's experiences within that world, and these ideas subsequently impact upon the content of laws (ibid.:41).

Consistent with the position that law is a creation rather than a reflection, Chambliss (1986:44) proposes that "people in particular historical contexts determine the content of law." Moving beyond both "normative" and "ruling-class" theories of law, he argues that law reflects

> a *dialectical process, a process through which people struggle and in so doing, create the world in which they live.* The history of law in capitalist countries indicates that in the long span of time, the capitalists fare considerably better in the struggle for having their views and interests represented in the law than do the working classes; but *the shape and content of this law is nonetheless a reflection of the struggle* and not simply a mirror image of the short run interests and ideologies of the "ruling class" or of "the people" (Chambliss 1986:49, emphasis added).

This quotation suggests that all individuals, dominant and subordinate, are implicated in the law creation process. Thus, while constructing laws to solidify their positions of dominance, law-makers cannot ignore the agency of those in the less powerful positions. As Collins (1982:27) notes, rulers are not always free to pass legislation from which they will benefit. Depending upon the strength of resistance by subordinate groups, proposed laws can be modified or even held back. It is therefore necessary to recognize that

> the legitimatory role of law, while real and important, is also fragile and volatile; its effects are not guaranteed, nor do they operate in the same way with all classes, movements and social groups. Legal legitimation competes with both rival legitimations . . . and with counter-hegemonic ideologies. . . . (Hunt 1991:117)

By emphasizing the role of the subject in the creation and transformation of law, the above discussion alludes to law's relational quality. Marx discusses the notion of relations in the *Grundrisse*:

> Society does not consist of individuals, but expresses the sum of interrelations, the relations within which these individuals stand. . . . To be a slave, to be a citizen are social characteristics, relations between human beings A and B. Human being A, as such, is not a slave. He [sic] is a slave in and through society. (1973:265)

Drawing on these ideas, Hunt (1991:105) defines law as a specific form of social relation. Law then, is not merely "an external mechanism of regulation but . . . a constituent of the way in which social relations are lived and experienced" (Hunt 1985:15-16; see also Althusser 1969:233).[4]

Whether structurally- or relationally-based, there has been a tendency in Marxist analyses of law to, *in the last instance,* award priority to the concerns of class. However, the process through which laws are constructed or transformed becomes more complex when one acknowledges that differences exist among individuals *within* social classes—for example, on the basis of "race" and gender—and these differences significantly impact upon the nature of law. Marxists have been criticized for their economic emphasis (see for example, Polan 1982; MacKinnon 1987; Smart 1991), largely because this exclusivity precludes adequate consideration of the law in relation to other oppressive social relations, such as those defined by gender or "race." With respect to law, then, Marxists might more appropriately ask: "What part, if any, does law play in the reproduction of *structural inequalities of class, race, and gender* which characterize capitalist societies?" (Hunt 1991:102, emphasis added) The work of Cathrine MacKinnon (1982, 1987) is one attempt to address the omissions of Marxists.

Law and the Perpetuation of Patriarchy

Written from the perspective of radical feminism, MacKinnon's work explores the oppression of women within the context of "meta-narrative" or a master theory approach—that is, she attempts to "account for everything in relation to one mode of explanation" (Smart 1991:138). Given this particular framework, I would argue that although she criticizes Marxism, MacKinnon is guilty of perpetuating similar problems of omission in her work. She criticizes Marxists for reducing explanations of exploitation and oppression to class terms, thereby overlooking the unique experiences of gender oppression. MacKinnon, however, is equally reductionist in her analyses of women's oppression.

For instance, MacKinnon (1982) constructs an argument about the oppression of women that very much parallels Marx's exploration of the oppression, exploitation and alienation of workers. Work however is replaced by sexuality: "Sexuality is to feminism what work is to Marxism: that which is most one's own, yet most taken away" (MacKinnon 1982:515). Sexual oppression, then, becomes the foundation of women's oppression. As Smart highlights, one of the difficulties with MacKinnon's position is the notion that *all* women share this experience of oppression and "that what women have in common is more significant than their differences" (Smart 1991:140).

The fundamental problem with focusing on sexual oppression in such a universalistic way is that the category "woman" becomes homogenized. MacKinnon's work is unable to adequately account for different oppressive experiences among women. One must, for example, explore the relationship between racism and sexism in order to better appreciate the distinctive oppressive experiences of Black women and women of colour (see for example, Davis 1983; hooks 1981; Giddings 1984). This problem of simply exploring oppression within the context of a male/female dichotomy is equally evident in MacKinnon's work on the law.

Law is conceptualized as an extension of the state and

> *the state is male* .... [T]he law sees and treats women the way men see and treat women. The liberal state coercively and authoritatively

constitutes the social order in the interest of men as a gender through its legitimizing norms, relations to society and substantive policies (MacKinnon 1987:140).

This argument is concretized with the example of rape, where MacKinnon essentially argues that "the law reflects the male understanding of [rape—i.e., just having sex/no intent], rather than the experience of the woman who has been violated" (Smart 1991:141; for a more detailed discussion of the rape example, see MacKinnon 1987:141-47).

The significance of MacKinnon's work undoubtedly is the challenge that it poses to the doctrine of the Rule of Law. As Smart notes, this analysis reveals that

> the problem [of law] is not going to be successfully tackled without challenging the fundamental principles of neutrality, objectivity and meaning (knowledge) . . . . [MacKinnon] is therefore not concerned with concepts of equality and fairness; instead she is concerned with *how male power is exercised in the guise of neutral and objective standards of the law* (1991:141, emphasis added).

Given her use of meta-narrative, however, there is little room within her argument to explain other oppressions. One cannot simply subsume "race" and class experiences within the more general category of gender oppression. Thus, as Smart (ibid.) asks: "how much of an advance is her conclusion that law . . . is male on the earlier (vulgar) Marxist analysis that law is bourgeois?"

Attempting to construct a feminist jurisprudence from the standpoint of women's experiences is a challenging process, for it necessitates equal recognition and legitimation of a multiplicity of experiences. There is no *one* woman's experience that can shape the nature of law any more than there is *one* master experience based on class or racial oppression. The problem therefore is twofold—to find a space within jurisprudence for all silenced experiences and to determine "what is to be done when different experiences conflict" (ibid.:155). The work of Polan provides one explanation for the way in which those in positions of power cope with conflicting experiences.

The Duality of Law

While Polan's work does not deal with the interplay of class, gender *and* "race," she does explore the interrelationship between class and gender within law and the way(s) in which law perpetuates both economic inequality and patriarchal forms of oppression.

Polan agrees with the stance of critical legal theory—that law does not operate "neutrally, ahistorically, or independently of the underlying power relations in society" (1982:294). Critical legal theory thus focuses on how the legal system supports a social order that is simultaneously capitalist, male supremacist (Polan 1982:295) and racist.

Critically exploring law from a Marxist-feminist perspective, Polan focuses on the:

> interaction of capitalism and patriarchy in maintaining women's oppression in modern society . . . demonstrat[ing] that the oppression of women has not remained static over time, but has changed historically in a dialectical relationship to changes in economic and social development and related changes in the role of the family. (1982:296)

Polan's work is particularly useful for highlighting how, at the ideological level, law facilitates the maintenance of exploitive relations between class- and gender-based groups. Specifically in reference to patriarchy, emphasis is placed on how the private/public dichotomy continues to be used, within the context of law, to legitimize the natural differences between men and women that have traditionally been used to oppress women (Polan 1982:298-99). The ideological manipulation of laws related to the public/private split serve a particular hegemonic function. Consider, for example, laws related to contraceptive use and abortion.

In the mid-twentieth century in the United States, a number of restrictions around contraceptive use and abortion were struck down through a series of Supreme Court decisions which declared as unconstitutional state interference into people's private sexual lives (Polan 1982:299). These kinds of decisions are generally perceived to be gains for women. However, by reinforcing the notion that the private sphere is outside the realm of state regulation these decisions might simultaneously have a negative implication/impact[5]:

> While the outcome of the birth control and abortion cases was beneficial to women by giving at least some women greater control over their reproduction, these decisions must also be understood as serving a hegemonic function, by legitimating the notion that there are naturally separate private and public spheres of human existence. (Polan 1982:299)

Clearly, highlighting differences among people can have both positive and negative ramifications for those who have been differentially identified and classified in relation to a norm or societal standard. Specifically, the notion of difference is used to assign individuals to categories and these categories determine "whom to include and whom to exclude from political, social and economic activities" (Minow 1990:21).

Like the treatment of sexism, Marxist approaches to the question of racism leave one with a sense of incompleteness. They either

> collaps[e] racism into a problem of class domination generally . . . as if it were nothing more than a consequential accident of evolving capitalism . . . *or* . . . [treat] racism as a mode of oppression so autonomous from capitalist social and economic relationships that it can be blamed on oppressors who appear as a classless "white society" . . . . (Freeman 1982:107)

Towards better appreciating the interaction between capitalism and racism, Freeman analyzes civil rights legislation in the United States. Emphasizing the duality of law, Freeman suggests that anti-discrimination law can rationalize, rather than ameliorate the problem of racial discrimination within society. He outlines arguments that can be used by those in positions of power to explain the persistence of racial discrimination in society, even after discrimination had been rendered illegal in codes of law (1982:97-99). Freeman refers to these explanations as the "victim" and "perpetrator" ideologies.

Very generally, the victim perspective argues that discrimination persists because visible minorities are not taking advantage of all of the new opportunities that the laws have created for them. This position is extremely problematic because it is based on the assumption that equality of opportunity is a reality rather than a myth. Because one can so easily expose the contradictions between the theory and the practice of equality of opportunity, this position is used less and less as a defence against discriminatory practices.

The perpetrator ideology, in contrast, does not deny that racial discrimination continues to be a problem. However, proponents of this position argue that the problem is not systemic. Rather, it is the result of the discrete actions of individuals or institutions that somehow become abstracted from the larger social structural framework. This position is a particularly convenient defence for those in positions of power for it implies that ". . . apart from the misguided conduct of particular actors, the rest of our society is working" (Freeman 1982:99). In other words, by focusing on individual violators of anti-discrimination laws, this perspective presupposes the achievement of a fair and equitable society. With the perpetrator perspective, the myth of equality of opportunity can be preserved. Thus, it is in the interests of those in positions of power to reject the victim perspective in favour of the perpetrator perspective (Freeman 1982:106-07).

The goal of civil rights law accordingly becomes

> to offer a credible measure of tangible progress without in any way disturbing the basic class structure. The more specific version of what would be in the interests of the ruling class would be to "bourgeoisify" a sufficient number of minority people in order to transform them into active visible legitimators of the underlying and basically unchanged social structure. (Freeman 1982:110)

The works of Polan and Freeman highlight the duality of law. In both cases, the authors demonstrate how legislative changes can be construed as gains for traditionally oppressed populations. However, in emphasizing the positive, the more negative hegemonic function served by these laws—i.e., to distract attention away from the structurally oppressive circumstances that continue to be perpetuated by those in positions of power—remains obscured.

Conclusion

Throughout this chapter, the role of law in reconstituting and legitimizing unequal social relations is explored. Considering law in relation to the hegemonic process, law is conceptualized as a dualistic, ideological discourse that is shaped by and reflective of dominant interests. Exposing this duality poses a serious challenge to the claim that law is a detached, objective, neutral expression of social values that transcends the immediate interests of individuals. Far from being detached, objective and neutral, law, as a creation of state actors, reflects the multiplicity of experiences of those who participate in the structures that rule. It must be emphasized however, that these law-makers and policy-makers operate within the context of highly structured, complex, bureaucratic institutions. In the creation of law and public policy, competing interests are acknowledged and negotiated through political process. Ultimately however, in making laws or formulating policy, these state actors are confined by the ideological, political and bureaucratic dynamics underlying the particular structures within which they are working (Knuttila 1992:165).

With the above in mind, I will proceed with a more substantive consideration of a particular piece of anti-discrimination legislation—the Canadian *Immigration Act*. But before turning to a specific consideration of the naturalization of racism in relation to Canadian immigration law, it is necessary to review, from a methodological standpoint, the stages through which the documentary analysis will unfold.

Notes

1. The idea of ideology as socially regulating is not unique to Marx. This notion is also prevalent in the work of other theorists, including Emile Durkheim. For an elaboration of his views, refer to Durkheim (1964a, 1965).
2. The way in which law is used to legitimate political authority is also discussed by Max Weber. According to Weber (1968), political legitimacy is based on "legal domination"—"the acceptance of governmental actions as legitimate insofar as they derive their authority from a legal order made up of an abstract and comprehensive system of rules" (Cotterrell 1992:154-55). For a more detailed discussion of Weber's conception of law in modern society, the reader is referred to Weber (1954, 1968).
3. For a comprehensive discussion of the Marxist approach to law, the reader is referred to Roger Cotterrell (1992:99-136).
4. For a perspective that similarly highlights law's relational quality, the reader is

referred to Silbey (1989).

5.   For a similar argument see Martha Minow's (1990:41) discussion of the potentially negative implications of special benefits for women.

3

Ideology as Methodology:
Documentary Analysis of Canadian Immigration Law

Introduction

In this book, the focus on "race" and marginality in relation to immigration law is designed to illuminate the problem of systemic discrimination towards visibly different immigrants. In Chapter Two, I dealt with the concept of ideology from a theoretical standpoint. I suggested that ideology assists in the reproduction, legitimation and naturalization of unequal social relations. I further submit that, when utilized by those in positions of power, ideology is illusory and socially regulating. Those who rule strive to regulate the production and distribution of ideas in a way that will protect their interests and positions of privilege. One might argue, then, that ideology is used to construct a particular version of social reality and social relations, and that this version identifies the special interests— for example, class interests, gender and/or racial standpoints—of its creators (Smith 1990a:32).

In this chapter, I will move beyond a theoretical exploration of ideology and its relationship to hegemony by considering *how* these versions of reality come to pass. Ideology, as it is expressed in documents/texts, is conceptualized as a method for furthering organizational interests—that is, the interests of those who rule (ibid.:45). To more concretely identify those ideological practices that are used to create hegemonic accounts of the social world, I will analyze federal government documents and their "accounts" of Canadian immigration. More precisely, I will examine how, from an organizational standpoint, immigration law and policies naturalize marginality among the "races." To construct knowledge from an organizational standpoint is to construct accounts that are "specifically detached from particular subjectivities" (ibid.::64). In doing so, "the objectified forms, rational procedures and the abstracted conceptual organization create an appearance of neutrality and impersonality that conceals class, gender and racial subtexts" (Smith 1990a:65). I approach my analysis of the organizational standpoint critically, highlighting how ideological practices within the social organization of immigration simultaneously conceal and perpetuate the problem of systemic racism. Before engaging in this research however, a methodological outline for guiding the documentary analysis must be created.

Documents, Discourses and the Social Construction of Reality

With the creation of discourse[1] from an organizational standpoint, comes an *appearance* of objectivity and neutrality that conceals class, "race" and gender subtexts. Throughout the documentary analysis, I shall highlight for the reader that objectivity within an organizational context is simply an appearance. The central question thus becomes: how are appearances maintained? A response to this question begins with ideology.

When addressing questions of ideology, it is customary to make reference to beliefs, ideas, images and symbols. It is also quite common to talk about ideology as a system of beliefs and/or ideas that shape one's vision of the social world. However, less frequently explored is the association of ideology with "a method of reasoning" (Smith 1990a:35). Before contemplating this association, it is necessary to contextualize the analysis to follow.

The documentary analysis takes as its starting point the "everyday world" of the organization. More specifically, I am focusing on the federal government organization that, in effect, manages Canadian immigration. In this sense, I am centring on an organization that, as part of "the ruling apparatus" (Smith 1990b:2), is mandated to reinforce and legitimize the existing relations of ruling. For some, an organization is an entity in and of itself. It represents a formal, bureaucratic structure that has been abstracted from, and somehow transcends, the individual. I argue instead, that it is a personification of the individual. The organization is comprised of people who occupy positions in the structures that rule. And, far from being detached, objective and neutral, these people "come to view the world in distinctive ways by virtue of their participation in the structures that rule" (Smith 1987:56). Thus, organizational accounts of immigration do reflect, albeit more subtly, the particular interests of those who participate in the ruling structure.

What then, is the everyday world of the organization? In the present context, I maintain that the everyday world of the organization appears before us in the form of documents. Furthermore, our knowledge of this world is, to a large extent, mediated by the various ideological discourses that appear within these documents. In order to strengthen and legitimize the positions of those who are part of this ruling structure, the documents direct us to think about and view the world within predetermined conceptual boundaries that are not disruptive to the ruling order. The generation of such accounts within government documents is integrally related to ideology as a methodological device.

Ideology as "A Method of Reasoning"

Ideology as a method of reasoning finds its roots in the work of Marx and Engels. They note that members of the ruling class rule as thinkers and producers of ideas by regulating the production and distribution of ideas at any given historical moment (Marx and Engels 1986:64-65). In order to prevail in a hegemonic struggle:

> each new class which puts itself in the place of the one ruling before it, is compelled, merely in order to carry through its aim, *to represent its interests as the common interests of all the members of society* ... it has to give its ideas the form of universality and represent them as the only rational, universally valid ones. (Marx and Engels 1986:65-66, emphasis added)

How, then, do specific interests come to be represented as common interests?

To begin, the version of reality embodied in organizational documents must reflect a generalized vision of or knowledge about the world, with which all societal members can identify. To create such an account, one can employ ideology as a method of reasoning. To reason ideologically is to engage in a process of "sorting out, and arranging conceptually, the living actual world of people" (Smith 1990a:42-43). Throughout the reasoning process, distinctive modes of interpretation evolve as a means of addressing "the juncture between the relations of ruling and actualities of people's lives that they organize and govern" (43). To facilitate the ideological process through which hegemonic accounts of reality come to be constructed, the following strategies are often utilized:

1) Ideas are detached from the people who say them and the circumstances in which they are said. In other words, ideas are detached from the real-world social relations in which they arise (Marx and Engels 1986:67; Smith 1990a:43, 39).

2) Once ideas are removed from the circumstances in which they were created, particular forms of argument and rhetorical modes are employed to design how actualities come to be inscribed (Smith 1990a:35) in the discourses of documents.

This ideological process is problematic because it generates a distorted conception of social reality. By confining to a conceptual level one's understanding of social reality, ideological methods of reasoning and the accounts that they produce "suppress the presence and workings of the underlying relations that they express" (37). In an effort to highlight the practical implications of this problem, this analysis will unravel documents pertaining to Canadian immigration law and policies. By looking at the ways in which forms of argument and rhetorical modes are incorporated into discourses that have racial implications, the study will bring to light counter-hegemonic interpretations of Canadian immigration documents. Through documentary analysis I hope to bring to the centre, knowledge that is customarily marginalized. As Martha Minow notes, "making central what has been marginal remakes the boundaries of knowledge and understanding and sheds new light on the whole" (1990:16).

Analyzing Racial Discourse—
A General Overview

The specific investigation of racial discourse in relation to Canadian immigration represents only one dimension of the more general process of capitalist state legitimation. Those in positions of power may utilize ideological discourses that explicitly or implicitly deal with racial matters in order to "persuade the population they are acting for the public good and in the general interest" (Reeves 1983:3). In relation to this legitimation process, it is imperative that the underlying dynamic of capitalism be recognized. However, what must also be acknowledged is that

> the contending classes pursue their interests at different institutional and discursive levels. The actual content of any example of racial or racist discourse is likely to reflect the true complexity of the decision-making process in which politicians seek to maximize a whole range of benefits and to minimize losses. (Reeves 1983:3)

Towards illuminating this complexity, my analysis substantively focuses upon a particular kind of discourse—that which has been ideologically "deracialized"—that is, a discourse which makes no explicit use of racist or racial categories but which nevertheless may, and often does, have racist effects (ibid.:4). In studying the content of these deracialized discourses, it is necessary to first locate the discourse within a particular social and historical context.

For example, in the forthcoming analysis I will be exploring, at a discursive level, the practical implications of two particular amendments to Canada's *Immigration Act*—the *Live-In Caregiver Program* and Bill C-86. To truly appreciate the logic underlying these amendments I must first identify the social and historical circumstances within which they arose. Subsequently, I will explore the arguments put forth to justify the legislative changes. Throughout the exploration, emphasis will be placed on: (1) interpreting the meaning of the discourses; (2) noting the recurrent themes within the discourses; and (3) identifying the techniques of persuasion used throughout the discourses. It is stressed throughout that, while a deracialized discourse is defensible against accusations of racism, "it is capable nevertheless of justifying racial discrimination by providing other non-racist criteria for the differential treatment of a group distinguished by its racial characteristics" (Reeves 1983:4).

Ideological Deracialization

In his analysis of the use of "race" in British political discourse, Reeves contends that there is a tendency on the part of government officials to deracialize situations which, to a social observer, either appear to be racist or may be judged to be racially discriminatory in their consequences. More precisely, ideological deracialization refers to "the attenuation of, elimination of, or substitution for racial categories in discourse, the omission or deemphasis of racial explanation and the avoidance of racial evaluation and prescription" (Reeves 1983:177). Deracialization is referred to as "asynchronic" where, in practice, there is evidence of racial domination, oppression and conflict but, at the discursive level, there is an avoidance of the term "race." Recall, as an example, the *Continuous Journey Stipulation* of 1908, the regulation by which the Canadian government excluded potential immigrants from India without ever using the word "race" or nationality in its discourse (see Chapter One this volume).

In relation to the process of ideological deracialization, the logic of "sanitary coding" is particularly effective. Sanitary coding is "the ability to communicate privately racist ideas with a discourse publicly defensible as non-racist" (Reeves 1983:190). Regarding immigration, one of the most effective coding techniques is "equivocation" (190-95). Briefly, equivocation involves the use of purposely vague and misleading terms in order to make the meaning, purpose or intent of some claim deliberately ambiguous or confusing. As an illustration, consider Dummett's analysis of the phrase "controlling immigration":

> At all times the propaganda in favour of "controlling immigration" has been understood on every side to mean "cutting down on coloured immigration," yet as with the wording of the law itself the defender of control can exclaim indignantly that he [sic] never mentioned colour but only the number of people coming into the country: while if he is attacked from the right, he can point out that everyone understood his remarks to refer to coloured immigration. (1973:185)

Along with the rhetorical mode of equivocation, there are also various "forms of argument" that expedite the process of ideological deracialization (Reeves 1983:204-39). As a justification for controlling immigration, the "populist," the "economic" and the *"pro bono publico"* forms of argument are particularly effective:

(1) *"Controlling immigration" is a popular measure.* This is known as the populist argument. The populist argument is one that allows the politician to pass the buck or avoid taking responsibility for the injustices being perpetrated against a particular target group of immigrants. For example, controlling immigration may go against the conscience of the politician but, if it is the will of the people, this will takes precedence over conscience. Thus, politicians may use the following kinds of phrases to justify controlling immigration: "I've received thousands of letters"; "the feelings of the people"; "From the Gallup Poll last week, there is no doubt where the public stands on this issue" (Reeves 1983:224-26).

(2) The economic argument takes this form: "There is a shortage or maldistribution of resources; obviously therefore, Canadian citizens should

have first access to resources." Within this context, the nature of immigration and the social construction of the immigrant is very much shaped by the economic conditions of the time. If a country is prospering and there are job vacancies, immigrant labour may be seen as necessary and the immigrant would represent a "positive" addition to the community. Alternatively, in more economically taxing times, the immigrant is characterized as "a burden on society and its resources" (Reeves 1983:227-28).

(3) The *pro bono publico* (also known as simply *pro bono*) justification is reflected in the statement: "All or most of the members of a community would "gain" from the change." In relation to controlling immigration, arguments of this type use the following kinds of logic—"the people will benefit from the measure"; "the greatest good for the greatest number will be served" and so on. Often, the purported gains for all are left unspecified. In other instances, *pro bono publico* may overlap with other forms of argument, e.g., economic. Consider the following example. Blacks in Britain would gain from immigration control, because control would facilitate the more equitable (re)distribution of resources among citizens. Blacks outside of Britain would also benefit by being prevented from coming into appalling urban conditions. This kind of control would also be beneficial to the whole, according to the logic of this form of argument, because it would reduce the prejudicial attitudes of whites towards Blacks. Corresponding to this circularity, the prejudice is reduced by excluding the cause of the prejudice—the actual immigrant (Reeves 1983:231).

In order to illustrate the use of various forms of argument and rhetorical modes in relation to the process of deracialization, I will analyze minutes from both House of Commons debates and from meetings of the Standing Committee on Labour, Employment and Immigration, as they pertain to two particular amendments to the *Immigration Act*. Introduced as immigration controlling measures, the amendments to which I am referring are the *Live-In Caregiver Program* and Bill C-86—the first major revision of the *Act* since 1976. In Chapter 4, I will first consider the case of the foreign domestics in Canada.

Note

1. To clarify, discourse, here and throughout this book, refers to spoken or written material.

4

Amending the Canadian Immigration Act:
The Live-In Caregiver Program

Introduction

The process through which laws are constructed and reconstructed is dialectical, that is, the content of laws changes in response to individual and collective experiences and struggles that occur within specific historical contexts. On matters pertaining to human rights, legislative changes may be defined as gains for the less advantaged populations. However, these gains can simultaneously benefit those in positions of power by subtly reinforcing already-existing structural or systemic forms of inequality. This duality of law is particularly evident in various forms of anti-discrimination legislation—including Canada's *Immigration Act.*

Historically, in relation to Canadian immigration, substantial gains have been made by less advantaged/minority populations. In principle, the law has moved from being restrictive to non-discriminatory. This principle of equality is now embodied in Section 3(f) of the *Immigration Act.* But even with this literal gain enshrining principles of equality, objectivity and neutrality, numerous accounts (e.g., Abella 1982; Malarek 1987; Whitaker 1987; Silvera 1989) provide continued evidence of racism and sexism in relation to Canada's immigration practices. These accounts suggest that there are obvious contradictions between the ideological principles and the practices of immigration. This chapter, however, does not conceptualize the problem as one of contradictions. Instead, towards better appreciating the persistence of discrimination within immigration, it explores the interplay between the text of law and "law talk." Put another way, this chapter analyzes the interplay between law and policy formation.

In general, there are two schools of thought under which existing studies of Canadian immigration policy might be classified—the "productive forces" model and the "state power" model (Simmons and Keohane 1992:425). In the case of the former, immigration policy is seen to be shaped solely by the forces of production and in the interests of the economic elite (e.g., Corbett 1957; Green 1976; Satzewich 1991; Stafford 1990). The latter, emphasizing the agency of state actors, conceptualizes the state as "a body with considerable scope for setting [immigration] policy within any constraints imposed by productive forces" (Simmons and Keohane 1992:425; for examples of this orientation, see Hawkins 1988; Dirks 1977; Matas and Simon 1989). However, to focus solely on either structure (productive forces) or agency (actors) in

46

analyses of Canadian immigration policy is to underestimate the complexity of the state's ongoing quest for legitimacy.

Towards acquiring legitimacy, the state actively pursues measures designed to satisfy a diversity of interests—labour and capital, ethnic groups and humanitarian organizations, to name just a few. In analyzing the interplay between the deracialized text of law and law talk, this part of the discussion will highlight the ways in which such diversity can be accommodated. I will begin by exploring the process of ideological deracialization in relation to Canada's *Live-In Caregiver Program*. Emphasis will be placed on how law, as a text, produces competing messages, thereby enabling racial discrimination to persist.

The Case of Foreign Domestics —Background Information

. . . sometimes I feel like a slave, sometimes I dream about freedom . . . . ("Noreen" in Silvera 1989:20)

All they want to do is work you like a slave and as soon as anything happen to you . . . that's it. They want no part of you. . . . We're doing dirty jobs. They are paying the money. But they think probably we are nobody. They must treat us equal, like we are human beings too, not like some animal. ("Molly" in Silvera 1989:66-70)

The above two excerpts, describing the experiences of two domestics working and living in Canada, are drawn from the oral histories of two Caribbean women. Perhaps most obviously, they sensitize us to the degree of exploitation foreign domestics have endured since their initial arrival in Canada in 1910 (Calliste 1991:141).

Black women began coming to Canada from economically "stagnant Caribbean countries to satisfy the need for cheap domestic labour" (Silvera 1989:vi; Calliste 1991:136-37). Formally entitled the *Domestic Scheme* and later the *Foreign Domestic Movement Program*, the first full-scale recruitment of West Indian women began in 1955 (Silvera 1989:7). To qualify, one was expected to be "young, of good character" (Bolaria and Li 1988:201), "single and without children" (Silvera 1989:vi).[1] These women were admitted as landed immigrants, but "could not go on to other work before spending at least one year as a domestic servant" (Bolaria and Li 1988:201).

Because of its unrewarding and exploitive nature, domestic work was generally abandoned by women as soon as possible and they became part of the larger reserve army of labour in search of other work (Silvera 1989:8). This was certainly of "no economic benefit" to the Canadian government but, rather than improving working conditions as incentive to stay in the occupation, the government chose to change its immigration policy towards domestic labour.

In 1973, women were admitted to do domestic work on non-immigrant temporary employment visas (TEVs). Unlike previous plans, domestics were not automatically entitled to landed immigrant status. Rather,

> each visa is issued for a particular kind of job, for a specific employer and for a definite period of time. If any of these circumstances change, the holder of the visa must immediately report to the Employment and Immigration Commission or run the risk of being deported. (Silvera 1989:8)

In 1981, under the *Foreign Domestic Movement Program*, regulations emerged allowing women to apply for "permanent residency" in Canada if they had been in the country for two years. The application process was complicated however, by the immigration officer's use of discretion. Officers were awarded the discretionary power to consider the woman's "aptitude for learning, . . . adaptability to Canadian lifestyle and personal suitability" (Silvera 1989:11).[2] It is politically advantageous to award discretionary powers to immigration officers because it provides a means for rationalizing problems of discrimination. Specifically, by using a "perpetrator perspective" (see discussion in Chapter 2), those in powerful positions will acknowledge the persistence of racial discrimination, but will argue that the problem is individualistic rather than systemic. The problem of racial discrimination is thus explained away in terms of the discrete actions of an individual—that is, the immigration officer.

The conditions attached to the TEV, in combination with the difficulties accompanying applications for permanent residency, discouraged women from challenging their often intolerable working conditions and various forms of physical and psychological abuse. Realistically, the Black domestic worker on a TEV was nothing more than a legal slave, imported to temporarily work in the homes of well-to-do Canadian families (Silvera 1989:5). As the Task Force on Immigration Practices and Procedures reports:

> their employment authorization is limited to employment with a designated employer, a person's status may change to that of visitor if she loses or gives up her job while in Canada. A visitor cannot apply for another employment permit from within Canada. This puts a high premium on clinging to one's job and leaves the domestic extremely vulnerable to exploitation. (1981:26)

Feeling powerless to confront their employers, these foreign domestic workers become docile, compliant and obedient (see "Primrose"; "Molly"; "Hyacinth"; and "Julie" in Silvera 1989). Furthermore, their tenuous legal status and work arrangements leave these women in constant fear of random deportation.

Whether this fear of deportation becomes reality is very much influenced by the economic context/climate at the time.

For example, the deportation of domestics who had arrived from Guadeloupe in 1911 occurred between 1913-15. During this period, Canada was in a recession and there were purported to be "scores of unemployed [Canadian] women who were willing to do domestic work" (Calliste 1991:142). A similar situation arose in the late 1970s when Canada once again faced a period of economic decline, with local unemployment levels at all-time highs. A widely publicized case during this period was that of "The Seven Jamaican Mothers" (see Silvera 1989:vi-vii; Calliste 1991:151), who were rounded up, charged with fraud and issued deportation orders. It was generally believed that this attack on domestics was "part of a policy to appease those uninformed Canadians who erroneously believed that Black immigrants were denying jobs to the unemployed" (Silvera 1989:vii).

In 1989, the *Foreign Domestic Movement Program* once again came under review. Although partially in response to charges of exploitation by domestic workers, the review was also designed to "ensure that the labour market need for live-in domestics was being met . . . and to respond to the concerns of employers about job changing and the quality of care" (House of Commons, Minutes of Standing Committee on *Labour, Employment and Immigration* (henceforth LEI) 8:7). From this review of the *Foreign Domestic Movement Program* emerged a number of important conclusions. Very briefly, the study concluded that: (1) in Canada, there was a need for live-in but not live-out caregivers and, accordingly, domestic workers should only be recruited to fill the need for live-in work; (2) some domestic workers are being exploited; and (3) after obtaining their status as permanent residents, most domestics (80 percent) leave in-home caregiving, enter the general labour market and "fare poorly in the general labour market" (LEI 8:8). The government response to this review was the *Live-In Caregiver Program*.

The Live-In Caregiver Program: Exploring the Interplay between the Text of Law and Law Talk

On January 30th, 1992 modifications were made to the *Foreign Domestic Movement Program*, renamed the *Live-In Caregiver Program*. Once again, the economic context within which these changes emerged must be noted. Canada was in a period of deep economic recession and unemployment was increasing steadily and dramatically. Economically, Canadians were and continue to be feeling progressively more threatened by outsiders who come to Canada and work for very low wages at undesirable jobs. As pointed out in Chapter 1, these outsiders historically have included those who are visibly different. It is therefore not surprising that annual reports by the Canadian Human Rights Commission have indicated growing racial intolerance "on many fronts" in

Canada (Vienneau 1990).

It is within this climate of economic instability and a growing culture of racial intolerance that the *Live-In Caregiver Program* was introduced by the Conservative government. At a discursive level, the program was presented to the Standing Committee on Labour, Employment and Immigration as an amendment that was both non-discriminatory and beneficial to the Canadian economy.

Laura Chapman[3] (Director General, Policy and Program Development (Immigration), Department of Employment and Immigration) had the following opening comments on the new program:

> Our view is that this is a very *complex* program, as are all aspects of the immigration program. We've tried to address the concerns of domestic workers by reducing the risk of exploitation. We've tried to ensure high-quality care and provide these workers with a realistic chance to succeed in the changing Canadian labour market. We think this program has succeeded in doing so, and I think that once this program is in place in a few weeks time *it will benefit everyone* (LEI 8:10, emphasis added).

To varying degrees, these changes have been criticized for reinforcing prejudice and systemic forms of discrimination (see for example, Nunziata/ Chapman, LEI 8:13-14; Serafico, LEI 8:17-18; Velasco LEI 8:19-20; and Bals, LEI 8:22-25). The comments of Pura Velasco (President, INTERCEDE, Toronto Organization for Domestic Workers' Rights) summarize quite succinctly the sentiments of foreign domestics affiliated with INTERCEDE:

> these changes are regressive for domestic workers and discriminate against women from Third World countries who make up the majority of participants in the Foreign Domestic Movement program. . . . Although these changes were presented as providing a response that balances the concerns of both domestic workers and employers, it is clear that these changes *only worsen the already discriminatory conditions for foreign domestic workers.* (LEI 8:9, emphasis added)

These negative sentiments were voiced largely in response to the announcement of two major and extremely controversial changes regarding criteria for entry into the program:

> entrants would be required to have completed the *equivalent* of a Canadian grade 12 education and to have taken at least six months of training in a field related to caregiving, whether that be the care of children, the elderly or the disabled. . . . (LEI 20:3, emphasis added)

Arguably, these changes represent a case of "asynchronic ideological deracialization" (Reeves 1983:177). Discursively, there is an elimination of or substitution for racial categories and a deemphasis of racial explanation. Practically, however, there is still evidence of systemic discrimination against Third World women of colour. Chapman made the following remarks on these issues:

> We also concluded that raising the education requirement to grade 12 equivalency would *not adversely affect any areas of the world*. To give you an example: the Filipinos now represent close to 60% of the total movement of foreign domestics; Jamaica represents approximately 5%; the U.K. approximately 7%; and other European countries approximately 21%. . . . Of those who enter from the Philippines now, 70% have grade 12 equivalency. Many people who are applying to Canada have and can meet those requirements. . . . Requiring formal training of six months *would also not adversely affect the world areas*, because countries provide a variety of caregiving or care-related courses, which could be incorporated into the training. That is, in the course of education up to grade 12 the individual could take caregiving courses. Homemaking courses are common in most countries. In addition, special courses are available and a number of countries have indicated that, in their view, they have opportunities for such courses and will be prepared to create others. Supervised, full-time, in-home care would also qualify as training. (LEI 8:8-9, emphasis added)

It is necessary to provide this and other rather lengthy excerpts from the LEI minutes in order to highlight the process of ideological deracialization—that is, the way(s) in which Chapman, through discourse, justifies these changes as non-discriminatory. The excerpts and analysis to follow will focus on the issues of grade twelve equivalency and six months of training in a field related to caregiving. Emphasis throughout will be placed on two things: (1) the lack of reference to "race"; and (2) the way(s) in which *pro bono* and economic forms of argument, as well as deliberately ambiguous terminology, are used to further perpetuate already-existing systemic discrimination. With this framework in mind, a more careful consideration of Chapman's opening remarks is in order.

In her opening description, Chapman describes the program as "complex," but one that "will benefit everyone." This *pro bono* form of argument is reinforced in her comments on grade twelve equivalency and six months of formal training in which she twice repeats that the formal introduction of these requirements "would not adversely affect any areas of the world." While Chapman is clearly trying to convince us that both Canadians and domestics will benefit from the pending changes to the domestic program, a number of questions arise from her remarks.

Regarding grade twelve equivalency, for example, one might ask what is equivalent to a grade twelve Canadian education in the various affected countries? And, if all possible cases cannot be specified, who will have the discretion to decide what constitutes equivalency? Furthermore, although Chapman claims no countries will be adversely affected by this change, she selectively chooses statistical information to support her case. She lists four areas from which domestics come to Canada—the Philippines, Jamaica, the United Kingdom and other European countries. She even includes approximate percentages that come from each area. However, when providing percentages on educational equivalency she only refers to the Philippines. One merely assumes that her concluding statement—"many people who are applying to Canada have and can meet those requirements"—is meant to describe the situation of the three other areas. While this statement may be sufficient for some, two questions automatically come to my mind: what exactly is meant by "many people" and why have specific percentages been omitted for the other three listed areas? Could it be perhaps that those percentages would reveal that some areas *are* adversely affected by these changes? According to Velasco (INTERCEDE) the answer to this latter question is definitively "yes":

> we are *firmly opposed* to the new educational requirement of Canadian grade 12 equivalence, which is the equivalent of Third World college education. This educational requirement is not consistent with the low-paid, low status nature of foreign domestic work in Canada. *This new educational requirement will restrict entry into the Foreign Domestic Movement of many women from Third World countries, particularly from rural areas, who are otherwise well-qualified in their skills and experience to be domestic workers.* (LEI 8:19-20, emphasis added)

Notwithstanding the sentiments of the domestic workers that are embodied in Velasco's statement, Chapman continues to defend her position in dialogues with various members of parliament. Let me first consider the Black/Chapman exchange.

Black/Chapman Exchange

> *Ms. Black (NDP/New Westminster-Burnaby)*: You have indicated that the department has done research on the availability of training in the major countries of origin for the Domestic Workers Program and that 70% of the applicants from the Philippines already had a grade 12 education at this point.

> *Ms. Chapman*: Grade 12 *equivalency* (emphasis added).

Ms. Black: But you did not give us the statistics for the people from Jamaica.

Ms. Chapman: From Jamaica, the proportion is over 50%. It has averaged between 50% and 55%.

Ms. Black: Has the department done any studies to show how accessible the 6 month courses are in those two countries in particular and what the accessibility to reach grade 12 equivalency is for the majority of the people in those two countries, particularly women?

Ms. Chapman: We have talked to representatives of those countries, who indicate that *grade 12 equivalency is reasonably accessible to those people.* I don't have actual numbers of graduates in grade 12 or equivalency for each country, but I could *probably* provide them for you in the future. (LEI 8:10-11, emphasis added).

Two things stand out in this exchange: the continued use of ambiguous terminology, like "equivalence," and the lack of reference to "race." First, the repeated use of ambiguous terminology is problematic. To this point it is unclear what constitutes grade twelve equivalency. In fact, only weeks before the program was to take effect, government officials were still unprepared to more precisely define the term. A Sub-Committee on Immigration, drawn from within the Standing Committee on Labour, Employment and Immigration, convened for the express purpose of studying the new changes to the domestic program. In its first report to the House of Commons on this issue, the sub-committee highlighted the potentially discriminatory effects of an imprecise use of the term:

> we are concerned that with the advent of the changes at the end of April, visa officers abroad may not have had, and may continue to lack, sufficient guidelines relating to both educational equivalencies and acceptable training courses. (LEI 20:4)

The ambiguity surrounding the six-month formal training requirement has correspondingly raised questions. In her opening remarks, Chapman argued that this requirement would "not adversely affect the world areas." In the same remarks she indicates that

> [h]omemaking courses are common *in most countries.* In addition, special courses are available and *a number of countries* have indicated that, in their view, they have opportunities for such courses and will create others. (LEI 8:9, emphasis added)

Once again, these remarks lack specificity. It is not clear what is meant by "most countries" or "a number of countries." In fact by reifying the notion of country, the ambiguity of Chapman's argument increases. Since a country itself cannot comment on availability, to whom is Chapman referring when she says "most countries"? Does she mean Canadian officials working in these countries or the country's own officials? No evidence is provided to elucidate the point. In fact, when Black questions Chapman about the accessibility of six-month training courses, Chapman does not acknowledge that part of the question in her response.

Why is Chapman so evasive about the issue of training courses? Would a direct response to questions about accessibility further discredit her argument that "no countries will be adversely affected by these changes"? Take the case of the Philippines as an example. According to Chapman, the majority of foreign domestics are Filipinos. She further contends that 70 percent of Filipinos now entering Canada have grade twelve equivalency. Clearly these statistics should encourage the reader, but for one problem. Grade twelve equivalency is not the only entry requirement. Six months of training in a field related to caregiving is also mandatory. Nowhere in Chapman's remarks is any reference made to the percentage of Filipinos (or any other group) who have completed such training. Could it be because the percentages are quite low? Or, could it be because such programs are virtually non-existent?

While this issue may not have been addressed by Chapman, it was raised by representatives of the domestic workers who presented briefs at the meeting. For example, Velasco (INTERCEDE) had the following comments on the six-month training program:

> [regarding] the requirement for six months of formal training in live-in care . . . it is discriminatory towards women in countries that do not offer such formal training programs. Such is the case in the Philippines, which currently provides the greatest number of workers in the FDM. In fact, this training does not exist in most Third World countries or in many European countries. *Overall, the impact of this new requirement is racist, in effect, for it will limit access to the FDM solely to women from developed countries and exclude women of colour from developing countries. . . .* (LEI 8:20, emphasis added)

In their report to the House, the Sub-Committee on Immigration reiterated the concerns of domestic workers:

> Domestic support groups maintained that training courses of this type are virtually non-existent in many traditional source countries. On this point, the government disagrees with the groups, suggesting that such courses do exist. The government was unable to offer us proof of this,

however, so we are unable to assess whether sufficient courses, in sufficient countries are available. (LEI 20:6)

Thus, the ambiguity and lack of specific evidence regarding accessibility of six-month training courses makes it difficult to discern, with any degree of accuracy, whether some areas are suffering adverse effects as a result of the new requirements. Within this context, ambiguity serves as an effective device for expediting the process of asynchronic deracialization.

What is interesting, albeit equally problematic, is the way in which discussions of accessibility unfold without reference to "race." This is particularly evident in the dialogues around the grade twelve equivalency requirement.

Within Chapman's opening remarks was an implicit suggestion that there is equal accessibility to grade twelve equivalency—i.e., "raising the education level to grade 12 equivalency would not adversely affect any areas of the world." Nowhere in these opening remarks was reference made to "races." However, when Black probed for more comprehensive statistical information on this point, the evidence revealed that one area in particular was negatively affected by the requirement change—Jamaica. Further statistical information was revealed in the Nunziata/Chapman exchange to highlight this point.

Nunziata/Chapman Exchange

> *Mr. Nunziata (Liberal/York South-Weston):* You indicated that 70% of Filipino domestics have the equivalent of grade 12 education. It's 50% to 55% for Jamaicans. What's the percentage for the U.K. and other European countries? . . .

> *Ms. Chapman:* I would think that it runs between 70% and 85%, depending on the country.

> *Mr. Nunziata:* Can you explain something for me? I am having some difficulty understanding this. What is the relationship between education and the ability to be a domestic or to have parenting skills? My mother raised seven kids and doesn't have a grade 12 education. I am just wondering how you relate education to the ability to do the work that the domestics come here to do.

> *Ms. Chapman:* I relate it to two things. I relate it to the quality of care in a very complex society and the fact that looking after children in our society is a very important job and one that I think we should place value on.
>
>   The other thing is equally important. . . . Most people do, in fact, leave the occupation after two to five years. They enter the mainstream

labour market. *We are not doing these people a favour if we bring them into this country and then leave them in jobs that are below the low-income cut-off* [emphasis added].

Mr. Nunziata: Just so I understand, are you saying the quality of care is diminished, depending on the level of education, so lesser educated women, for example, provide less quality of care for their children?

Ms. Chapman: No I'm not saying that. I'm saying that as an immigration officer it is often difficult to assess the intangibles. I can't look at any one of you and tell whether you are going to be a good or a bad caregiver. I have to assess the objective criteria.

The objective criteria we are prepared to look at are those that relate to things that we can test. Educational equivalency is one of those. Real training is another of those. We have to use criteria that can be applied in a systematic way across the world. We cannot use criteria based on feel.

Mr. Nunziata: Can you see that your policy is discriminatory when you examine the statistics you have provided for us in terms of the equivalency to grade 12?

Ms. Chapman: No, I don't think it's discriminatory. In fact, I think it is not at all discriminatory. What it does is bring people in and uses the same criteria for all parts of the world, and that is the way our immigration program works. We use exactly the same criteria. . . . If that means that more people come from India than other parts of the world, then that's it, because we do it on the basis of the same criteria.

Mr. Nunziata: Some people call that systemic discrimination. (LEI 8:13-14)

The statistics provided for the United Kingdom and other European countries—70 percent to 85 percent—further accentuate the adverse effects of this policy on a particular source country. It is therefore possible to conclude that the language may have been deracialized around this proposed program change in an effort to avoid or dismiss accusations of racism. But, in practice, the deracialized change clearly perpetuates the problem of systemic discrimination. It may be useful to further explore the Nunziata/Chapman exchange in order to highlight the ways in which Chapman strives to sell the changes as non-discriminatory.

To win support for grade twelve equivalency, Chapman utilizes a *pro bono* form of argument. She attempts to show how both the employer and employee would gain something from this new requirement. The employer would gain an employee who could better care for children in an increasingly complex society. Having heard testimony from both supporters and opponents to the *Live-In Caregiver Program*, the sub-committee established to study the proposed changes to the domestic program,[4] had the following to say:

> We do not agree . . . that a rigid requirement of grade 12 equivalency necessarily meets the needs of Canadian employers or caregivers or will result in the selection of the best candidates for the program. . . . *No amount of education can instill the warmth of personality necessary for caregiving.* Successful on-the-job experience, on the other hand, means that the Canadian employer can rely on the suitability of the caregiver for the work involved. (LEI 20:5, emphasis added)

Furthermore, the sub-committee questions making *mandatory* grade twelve equivalency, particularly since it is not a mandatory requirement of entry for those immigrants who are applying independently under the purportedly objective points system. Their argument is presented as follows:

> We note that this educational requirement does not apply to independent immigrants under the points system. Although points are awarded under the "education factor" for each grade completed up to grade 12, the latter level of achievement is not mandatory. The committee thinks that *the government should not mandate a higher level of education for participants in the Live-In Caregiver Program than that required for independent immigrants.* (LEI 20:5, emphasis added)

In relation to gains for the employee, Chapman argues that those who have achieved grade twelve equivalency would have better chances for success in the mainstream labour force—since most domestics leave the occupation after two to five years. Thus, according to Chapman's logic, by *not* imposing upon them a grade twelve equivalency requirement, "we aren't doing these people any favours." Once again, Chapman seems to overlook a very important point. According to the sub-committee:

> experience with the program over the last decade has shown that *caregivers are willing and able to improve themselves once they arrive in Canada* . . . . [I]f they have not attained grade 12 upon acceptance into the program, *participants should be given the additional two years in Canada to upgrade to a level of formal education suitable for entry into the regular labour market before being granted permanent residence in Canada.* (LEI 20:5-6, emphasis added)

It is possible for domestics to obtain grade twelve equivalency once in the host country—for example, through night school. Furthermore there is, at best, an ambiguous connection between education and quality of care. Why, therefore, does there seem to be such an insistence on grade twelve equivalency *prior* to arrival? Domestics themselves argue that in altering the caregiver program, the government should place less emphasis on making domestic workers more competitive in the general labour market. Instead, in order to encourage domestic workers to stay in the occupation, greater consideration should be given to ways of ameliorating the conditions which domestics are forced to endure within the homes where they are employed. According to Lorina Serafico, Steering Committee Member, West Coast Domestic Workers Association:

> what domestic workers are asking for is simply respect—respect for and recognition of domestic work as work of value. *The government should take the lead in respecting and recognizing domestic work as valuable work.* . . . If the government truly wants domestic workers to stay in domestic occupations, they must be ready to pass legislation to provide domestic workers with, among other things, higher pay, better working conditions, equal labour protection. The government must extend to domestic workers the respect and recognition they truly deserve. (LEI 8:16-17, emphasis added)

Interestingly, there was one organization that did support the implementation of the grade twelve equivalency requirement—the Canadian Coalition for In-Home Child and Domestic Care. The spokesperson for this organization, Marna Martin, had the following to say in her presentation to the Standing Committee on Labour, Employment and Immigration:

> I'm here on behalf of the Canadian Coalition for In-Home Child and Domestic Care, a national non-profit organization formed in 1987 to represent the concerns of employers, employees and agencies involved in the in-home placement industry and *to lobby the government for equitable solutions for all parties concerned.* . . .
>
> We support the government's decision to require applicants for the FDM program to have completed an educational level equivalent to grade 12 education in Canada. . . . Statistics show that over the next 10 years, 65% of all jobs in Canada will require a minimum of grade 12 education. All those who are issued work visas for Canada through the Foreign Domestic Movement program, are allowed to apply for landed immigrant status after successful completion of two years' live-in domestic work. Subsequently, they are allowed to enter the general labour market.

It would be an injustice to everyone concerned to allow workers into Canada who are unequipped to readily meet the demands of becoming self-sufficient after obtaining their landed immigrant status.

From our experience in the field, we have found that *there is a strong tendency for those who have at least this level of education to be better able to understand instruction and the underlying principles and be better equipped to handle emergency situations*; to be better able to deal with the language, discipline and development skills of Canadian children; to be better able *to provide stimulating play and educationally appropriate activities, as well as creative interaction* between themselves and Canadian children; be more stable employees with long terms of employment with their employers; be more easily integrated into Canadian society upon gaining landed status; to *be more easily employable once they are landed, as they have more background knowledge and skills to make them employable and are much less costly to the Canadian taxpayer, as they require fewer government-funded programs* . . . and finally, to be more able to access the system and be less vulnerable and intimidated in situations where they are being abused or wrongfully treated.

. . . *[W]e do not believe this policy is racist or discriminatory.* Indeed, our agency members report that the majority of their place-ments involve persons from the Third World. However, the Foreign Domestics Movement is *not an aid* to the Third World program; it *is a labour market policy for qualified caregivers.* (LEI 8:28-29, emphasis added).

I've provided such a lengthy excerpt from this particular agency's statement in order to highlight the similarities between the ideas of this organization and those of the government. The nature of this statement certainly seems to render questionable the claim that this organization represents the interests of *both* domestics and employers.

First, there is a *pro bono* argument being made by Martin when she suggests that "it would be an injustice to everyone concerned" to allow domestic workers to enter the country without grade twelve equivalency. She argues that because one can apply for landed status after two years as a domestic, and subsequently enter the general labour market, one will need grade twelve equivalency in order to cope with the new challenges one will face. Interestingly Martin, like the government, seems to overlook the fact that grade twelve equivalency could be obtained in the host country if conditions for live-in domestics were not so oppressive. Furthermore, she makes the assumption that all domestics want to leave the occupation. Martin emphasizes movement to the general labour market after two years, but does not discuss ways of making domestic work more competitive—that is, improving conditions for domestic workers to the point that they might actually *desire* to stay in the occupation for more than two years.

Martin also provides a very ethnocentric discussion of the links between childcare and education. Clearly representative of employers' concerns once again, her observations implicitly suggest that those without grade twelve equivalency (which coincidentally seem to cluster around particular geographic areas) are less able to "understand instruction . . . to handle emergencies . . . to provide stimulating play and educationally appropriate activity . . ." and so on. Interestingly, the sub-committee studying the changes to the *Live-In Caregiver Program* concluded that those with higher levels of education do *not* necessarily make the best caregivers—rather that successful previous on-the-job experience may be a better indicator of suitability for caregiving (LEI 20:5). However, we see no discussion of the value of on-the-job experience in Martin's remarks.

Finally, Martin ends her discussion with an argument that utilizes both *pro bono* and economic elements. As a labour market policy, the *Live-In Caregiver Program* must require grade twelve equivalency—it will make the caregivers less of a burden on Canadian taxpayers, for they will need fewer government-funded programs geared towards adaptation to Canadian life after obtaining their landed status. As for the worker, she will benefit by being less vulnerable in situations of abuse or wrongful treatment. How grade twelve equivalency reduces the likelihood of economic exploitation or various forms of physical, emotional, psychological or sexual abuse is less than clear.[5]

Given the discrepancy between this position and the positions presented by other domestic worker organizations, the following observation by Mr. Pagtakhan (Liberal/Winnipeg North) seems particularly interesting:

> *Mr. Pagtakhan*: I would like to pose my question to the Coalition for In-Home Child and Domestic Care, which is an association that includes, among others, the employees and the agencies. . . . First, how are you funded?. . . .

> *Ms. Martin*: We have absolutely no funding. Our only income is through membership fees paid on a yearly basis.

> *Mr. Pagtakhan*: How much is the membership fee for employees?

> *Ms. Martin*: For an employee it's $10 a year.

> *Mr. Pagtakhan:* For agencies?

> *Ms. Martin*: For employers it's $35 a year. For agencies the initial membership is $400, and then it's $200 a year thereafter.

Mr. Pagtakhan: With that structure of fees, would you not see a potential conflict of interest as you determine and present their case before the government?. . . [I]t is interesting that while most of the domestic workers would not like the grade 12 equivalency and have labelled the changes discriminatory and racist, your group has said it is not. So my question is, how do you purport to reflect the views of domestics, the very essence of the program, and say there is not a conflict of interest? But now you say you get a fee from the agencies manyfold higher. How do you explain that?

Ms. Martin: Well, our agency members represent thousands of employers and employees through the agency, so not necessarily all of their clients are separate members, as employers. There are many employers, of course, that don't go through agencies and they are separate members. (LEI 8:36)

Although the point of this dialogue may be self-explanatory, I would simply like to highlight how Martin's response to the question is deliberately ambiguous, and does not even address the issue of conflict of interest.

Conclusion

Throughout this discussion of the *Live-In Caregiver Program*, the process of deracialization has been illuminated. Debates around the issues of grade twelve equivalency and six months of specialized training highlighted how, without mentioning the word "race," legislative changes could be used to perpetuate already-existing forms of systemic discrimination. Beyond avoiding the term "race," deliberately ambiguous terminology was used in both the text of law and law talk, thereby rendering the meaning or intent of various claims confusing. Throughout the debates, the politicality of law becomes increasingly clear. Politicians, aiming to sell legislative changes to diverse constituencies, must at least provide the impression that, in the process of creating law and public policy, competing interests are acknowledged and negotiated. As the state vies for legitimacy, equivocation in both the text of law and law talk becomes an effective means for providing different responses to divergent interests.

Since the new regulations of the *Live-In Caregiver Program* came into effect on April 27, 1992, there has appeared evidence of discrimination, especially in relation to the controversial "six months of formal training relevant to the position being applied for" (Young 1994:19):

the Department found that most refusals under the program were arising from an inability to meet the training requirement; this was particularly so in Hong Kong and Singapore, where many Filipina applicants are well-educated and experienced but lack formal training. (Young 1994:19-20)

This point had been raised by domestic workers during the debates, but was ignored. Now faced with the evidence, the government was required once again to alter its policy. So in July of 1993, the training requirement was modified as follows: "applicants need *either* six months of training or 12 months of actual experience in the kind of caregiving work to be undertaken" (Young 1994:19, emphasis added).

To further accent the political nature of law and the power of equivocation, I now turn to a consideration of the interplay between the text of law and law talk in relation to Bill C-86.

Notes

1. Many women who applied to do domestic work in Canada already had children whom they were supporting. But, given the very precarious economic situations in their home countries, they were encouraged to omit this fact in order to avoid "being excluded from consideration" (Silvera 1989:vi).
2. Within the points system, "personal suitability" is worth only ten points out of a hundred, but the immigration officer's discretionary power extends well beyond this. As discussed in Chapter 1, Section R11(3) of the Immigration Regulations grants officers enough discretion to essentially override the points system (Employment and Immigration Canada 1991:07-90-6).
3. In her capacity as Director General, Laura Chapman is responsible for:
    the development of policies and programs relating to the number and classes of immigrants coming to Canada, the various types of temporary entrants ... restricting entry and ensuring the removal of undesirable persons, as well as all aspects of the settlement and integration of immigrants and refugees. (Law Society of Upper Canada 1993)
4. Interestingly, while the appointed sub-committee was studying the proposed changes to the *Foreign Domestic Program*, the "government proceeded to implement its new regulations which came into effect on 27 April 1992" (LEI 20:3). The fact that the government did not wait to hear the recommendations of the sub-committee is offensive to all those who participated in the process of reviewing the program—from the designated sub-committee members to the valued witnesses who came from across the country to speak for or against the proposed changes.
5. For documented cases of various forms of exploitation and abuse, and the "roadblocks" that are encountered when assistance is sought, see Silvera 1989.

    It should also be noted that the sub-committee studying the *Live-In Caregiver Program* urged the federal government to take a more active role in monitoring the implementation of the program throughout the provinces in order to ensure that caregivers are protected from abuse and exploitation. Once again, however, the reader is reminded that the government implemented the new program, *before* receiving the report from the sub-committee it appointed to evaluate the program.

5

Bill C-86:
Managing Immigration in the '90s

Introduction

Canada's current *Immigration Act* was passed by Parliament in 1976 and came into force in 1978. Prior to the introduction of Bill C-86 in June 1992, there had been no major revamping of the 1976 *Act* (Young 1992:1). In the prefacing comments to Immigration Canada's publication *Managing Immigration: A Framework for the 1990s*, Minister of Employment and Immigration Bernard Valcourt made the following comments in relation to the proposed changes to the *Immigration Act*:

> The proposed changes will allow us to continue to support family reunification, and to select immigrants in a manner more responsive to the economic and labour force needs of Canada. They will ensure that we can effectively protect Canadian society against those who would abuse our immigration program and the generosity of Canadians. And they provide for a more efficient, streamlined refugee determination system, ensuring that we can help those who truly need refuge in the fairest and most timely manner possible. (Immigration Canada 1992)

Bill C-86 is 124 pages in length and contains 131 clauses. This lengthy and complex piece of legislation, which "extensively amends" (Young 1992:1) Canada's *Immigration Act* (R.S. 1985 c.1-2), was first read in the House of Commons on June 16, 1992. The Bill was subsequently rushed through readings and debates in both the House of Commons and the Senate, receiving Royal Assent on December 17, 1992. The Conservative government's handling of Bill C-86 has generated much criticism and concern from many different Canadian constituencies. In general, the critics of Bill C-86 questioned the rush. Why was such an important and detailed amendment to immigration legislation being pushed through Parliament? Why, prior to the introduction of the Bill, had there been no consultation with organizations representing Canadians (e.g., Canadian Ethnocultural Council; the National Organization of Immigrant and Visible Minority Women of Canada; the Canadian Jewish Congress; The Canadian Labour Congress; the Inter-Church Committee for Refugees) who might be affected by these changes? Why was there minimal time for witnesses to prepare testimony on the changes? Why was time to debate the Bill and its finer points minimized?

I will deal with Bill C-86 in a way that highlights its effects as an immigration controlling mechanism. Again, the interplay between the text of law and law talk is examined in order to better appreciate the persistence of racial discrimination within immigration. Before proceeding, it is worth noting that the analysis of Bill C-86 will have a different emphasis than that of the *Live-In Caregiver Program*. The debates around the *Live-In Caregiver* legislation are specific in scope. Thus, in the context of deracialized texts, it is possible to highlight quite easily how *pro bono* and economic forms of argument and ambiguous terminology are used to perpetuate already-existing systemic discrimination against Third World women of colour. In the case of Bill C-86 however, the exclusionary potential of the *Act* is far more subtle, and this merits a variation on my earlier form of investigation.

My analysis begins with the assertion that an economic argument formed the foundation upon which Bill C-86 was built and sold to Canadians. The immigrant was socially constructed to be one who was abusive to, and a burden on, Canada and its resources. After setting the context within which Bill C-86 was introduced, the analysis will focus more exclusively on the logic of sanitary coding as it comes to be manifested in the technique of equivocation.

Contextualizing Bill C-86: Why the Need for Change?

As a preamble to the discussion on a new management framework that would emerge with Bill C-86, Meyer Bernstein (Director, Strategic Planning and Research, Department of Employment and Immigration) remarked on the nature of the foreign-born population in Canada:

> The bulk of the immigrants, roughly two-thirds are from Europe. But this has been changing very quickly. The major ethnic groups are still British, French, German and Italian, but if you look at the recent flows, roughly three-quarters are non-European and non-US. The result has been *a visible minority population that presently stands at 6% to 7%, but is expected to rise sharply*. In the two major immigrant receiving centres, Toronto and Vancouver, within a decade, the visible minority proportions are going to be roughly 40% to 45% (Bernstein in House of Commons 1992(3):7; emphasis added).

Bernstein continues by arguing that *thus far*, "the marriage between immigrants and Canada has been a happy one"—both economically and socially. But the more important question is "whether it will continue to be so." (ibid.) What the discussion seems to be suggesting is that, although immigration has succeeded in the past, its future success is in jeopardy. Specifically, Bernstein argues that

> [o]n many fronts we find that today's immigrants don't enjoy the advantages enjoyed by earlier cohorts. The educational advantage,

formerly enjoyed by foreign born, has largely disappeared, although we still import a significant number of highly educated and highly skilled people. The proportion of professionals and managers has dropped. Fewer immigrants are proficient in English or French and recent immigrants have been experiencing higher rates of unemployment and social assistance. In fact, there is mounting evidence of significant impact gaps and of a lengthening catch-up time period. There are even some signs suggestive of maladjustment in the form of rising criminality, although it is still well below the Canadian average (House of Commons 1992 (3):9).

The purpose of citing these two passages at length is to highlight, at the outset, that the Conservative government is clearly uncomfortable with the changing face of immigration in Canada. It is quick to characterize "the marriage" between Canada and its immigrants as successful, but the success seems to be linked, albeit implicitly, to the more traditional, white immigrant of the past. It is interesting that "today's immigrants" (the majority of whom are visible minorities) have come to be depicted as dependent, socially maladjusted people who are prone to crime. In reality, is there a link between the colour of one's skin and the ability to adapt successfully to life in Canada? Or are these problems simply mythical constructions on the part of the government, designed to facilitate the selling of Bill C-86 to Canadians? Here, the latter will be argued. To begin, consider the comments to Canadians from Immigration Canada.

From the perspective of Immigration Canada, there is a rather pressing need to develop new ways to "manage" Canada's immigration program, largely because "over the past decade, there have been growing, unpredictable, and large scale movements of people from one country to another" (Immigration Canada 1992:3).[1] Movement could occur for any number of reasons: people simply searching for a better life; people fleeing persecution, civil war, poverty and food shortages in home countries; and people being forced from their homelands as a result of natural or environmental disasters (Immigration Canada 1992:3-4). It is within this context that politicians are faced with the arduous task of ensuring that immigration continues to contribute to the well-being of all Canadians. At the same time, however, the "compassion and humanitarian values" (Immigration Canada 1993:3) that *in principle* lie at the heart of immigration programs must be protected. Immigration, therefore, must be based on principles of non-discrimination, and it must continue to support family reunification and a humanitarian concern for refugees. With this in mind, the immigration minister sets out to determine how to reorganize the immigration process in order to best respond to the social and economic needs of Canada.

From an economic standpoint, investors must be accepted *without limits* for the contributions that they can make to Canada's overall economic development

(Immigration Canada 1992:16). Immigration can further strengthen the economic well-being of Canada when immigrants are accepted to fill skilled employment positions for which there are no Canadians available. Immigrants can also enhance regional development in Canada by settling in areas where they can make the greatest contribution. What is problematic from an economic standpoint, however, is the overconcentration of immigrants in large metropolitan areas, for this can place excessive demands on the health, social and educational services that are available in these communities (Immigration Canada 1992:5).

According to Immigration Canada, ensuring the well-being of Canadians also necessitates that they be protected from those who "abuse the system." This includes protection from people who exploit the system once in Canada (e.g., welfare fraud) and those "criminals" and "terrorists" that may try to gain entry into our country with the intent of engaging in disreputable activities.

> An immigration program that is not properly controlled is vulnerable to abuses by criminals, terrorists and others who might jeopardize the safety and well-being of Canadians. In recent years we have seen the development of more organized, highly professional criminal networks intent on circumventing international and national laws. . . . As *the volumes* of people seeking to enter Canada increase, vigilance is needed to ensure that Canadian society is protected from those who are not welcome in our country and who are intent on breaking its laws. (Immigration Canada 1992:7-8, emphasis added).

Thus, to balance the needs of Canadians with Canada's reputation as a caring and compassionate nation, the Conservative government introduced Bill C-86. To understand the underlying logic of Bill C-86, it is important to get a sense of the political climate at the time of the Bill's introduction.

The Political Climate and Bill C-86

As noted previously, the face of Canadian immigration has changed dramatically over the past several decades, in favour of new immigrants from the Third World and away from traditional immigrants from Europe and the United States (de Silva 1992:8). To more clearly illustrate the meaning of *dramatically*, consider the following:

> In 1957, 95% of the 282,164 immigrants [to Canada] were Europeans or Americans. But of the 152,098 immigrants to Canada 30 years later, the percentage of Europeans and Americans had dropped to 24%. The remainder came mostly from the Third World. (Kopvillem 1990:40)

Very generally, the climate might be described as one in which Canadians are feeling far more vulnerable economically, are developing a growing sense of mistrust and intolerance towards outsiders, and are increasingly disillusioned and discontented with the government. Polls from both Gallup and Decima research lend support to these claims. According to the *Gallup Report* released on May 7, 1992, almost "6 in 10 adult Canadians cite some aspect of the economy as the most important problem facing the country today." More precisely, 34 percent of adult Canadians, as compared to 16 percent in 1989, cite unemployment as the most serious problem currently facing Canada (Gallup 1992a:2). In this same poll Canadians were asked, on a scale ranging from "very concerned" to "not at all concerned," how they felt about a number of contemporary Canadian issues—e.g., unemployment, taxation levels, abortion, treatment of natives, threat of nuclear war, senate reform, honesty in government, Quebec separation, free trade and Canadian unity. Once again, unemployment topped the list, with 80 percent of adults stating that they were "very concerned" about unemployment. Regarding the issue of faith or confidence in the government, 71 percent of adults said they were very concerned about "honesty in government." This ranked third on a list of concerns, after unemployment and taxation levels.

Similar kinds of findings can be found in the November 1992 poll conducted by Decima research for *Maclean's* magazine. When asked, "what is the most important problem facing Canada today," 64 percent of adult Canadians mentioned a problem related to the economy. More specifically, 39 percent of the population in 1992, as compared with 6 percent of the population in 1989, felt unemployment was the most serious problem. Twenty-five percent of the population in 1992, as compared with 10 percent in 1989, felt the economy/ recession was the most serious problem facing Canadians ("Voices of Canada" 1993:42).

There is also evidence from recent Gallup and Decima research polls supporting the idea that negative sentiments among Canadians towards outsiders—that is, immigrants and refugees—are increasing. The polls similarly suggest that people's levels of tolerance are tied to their feelings about the economy. A closer scrutiny of these findings begins with a review of *Maclean's* 1992 year-end poll. Results of the poll, as they pertain to immigration, are as follows:

1) "Canadians find it more difficult to accept new arrivals, particularly those from regions other than Europe or the United States" (Wood 1993:26).

2) Over the past two decades, regardless of age, income or level of education, only about one respondent in five welcomed the increase in immigration from Asia, the West Indies and other, mainly Third World, countries. The rest of the sample described immigration from these areas as either "bad," "very bad," or "simply a fact of life" (ibid.).

When these results are compared with respondents' views on the economy, the evidence suggests that the recession has affected people's attitudes towards immigration:

> 32% of those who were pessimistic about the economy had negative opinions of visible minorities while only 26% of those who felt that the economy was improving said that immigrants from Asia, the West Indies and other parts of the Third World were bad for Canada. (Wood 1993:26-27)

Finally from the *Maclean's* poll, we get a sense that Canadians are becoming less accepting of cultural difference. There seems to be a trend away from multiculturalism, as 64 percent (compared to 57 percent in 1989) of respondents felt that immigrants should be encouraged to "blend in with the larger society," rather than "maintain their distinct culture and ways" ("Voices of Canada" 1993:44). These trends towards increasing intolerance seem to be consistent with various findings from the *Gallup Report*.

For example, in a report released on May 25, 1992, the majority of Canadian adults, 54 percent, believed that there had been "an increase in racial intolerance over the last five years." When asked for future predictions, 67 percent felt that there will be an increase in racial problems over the next five years (*Gallup Report* 1992b:1). In a poll on immigration control released only a couple of weeks later it was found that

> almost one in two people (46%) believe that Canada should accept fewer immigrants at the present time. Only 13% of Canadians favour increasing the immigration level to the country, while 37% fully endorse the status quo. Another 4% offer no opinion concerning this controversial issue. (*Gallup Report* 1992c:1)

It should be noted that those above-mentioned findings, which suggest that prejudice and intolerance result from economic threat, are reinforced in studies conducted by the Economic Council of Canada (EEC) (1991a, 1991b). In its analysis of public opinion surveys on immigration-related matters, the EEC examined sixty-two different national surveys conducted by Gallup, Decima and Environics over the period 1975-90 (EEC 1991a:27). Most germane, in the present context, is the following finding:

> whenever there happened to be a coincidence of high or worsening unemployment and high proportions of visible minorities, unfavourable attitudes [towards immigrants] were much more likely to develop. (EEC 1991A:28; see also EEC 1991b:116)

Finally, on the question of attitudes towards the government, there were a number of questions in the *Maclean's* survey that are relevant. When Canadians were asked "what do you think has been the main reason for Canada's slow recovery from the recession," 43 percent felt it was because the federal government had done a poor job managing the economy. There was a tie for the second most popular response, with 20 percent of Canadians attributing the problem to "slow growth abroad" and 20 percent attributing it to the negative effects of the Free Trade Agreement with the United States ("Voices of Canada" 1993:42).

On the question of "faith in politicians to serve the public interest," 73 percent of respondents polled claimed that their faith in politicians had decreased; 42 percent felt it had "decreased significantly," and 31 percent felt it had "decreased somewhat" ("Voices of Canada" 1993:43). When asked why politicians are not regarded favourably, 67 percent seemed to question the commitment of politicians to their various constituencies. Specifically, 34 percent of those polled felt that politicians "spend too much time talking among themselves, and not enough time with the people," while 33 percent felt that their representatives in government "only seem interested in helping themselves and abusing their positions" ("Voices of Canada" 1993:43).

In this climate of growing intolerance, economic vulnerability and disillusionment with the government, the Conservatives were clearly facing a hegemonic crisis. How, with the introduction of Bill C-86, could the government try to regain the support and confidence of the people? Emphasizing the complementarity of law, it is argued that the government can take already-existing conditions, like the recession, high levels of unemployment and increasing racial intolerance, and use these conditions to its own advantage. The government begins by introducing Bill C-86 in a way that centres on abuses to the system by outsiders. In doing so, people's disillusionment with those in power temporarily subsides, as responsibility for the state of the nation shifts away from the government towards those who, arguably, are the most vulnerable in this situation—potential immigrants and refugees. If the government can convince Canadians that the source of their economic woes lies elsewhere—i.e, with the "abusing immigrant"—and that the government is determined to protect Canada from these opportunistic people, it may be able to regain some public support and confidence.

Immigration Minister Bernard Valcourt knew that, among many Canadians who were feeling economically threatened, there was a growing sense of mistrust and intolerance towards outsiders, particularly visibly different outsiders. Capitalizing on this, Valcourt cited various polls which suggested that Canadians were generally supportive of legislation that would more effectively control and regulate immigration. For example, Valcourt released a poll during the week of September 7, 1992, claiming broad Canadian support for his Bill. It said that 22% could be classified as xenophobes, those "very fearful about their future [who] see immigration as a threat, or perhaps a cause of their already marginal position in society." (Harper 1992:A24)

More detailed findings from January 1992 were also presented and used by the government to defend Valcourt—that is, to reinforce the idea that Bill C-86 put Valcourt and the Conservatives "on the right track" with Canadians. From this "immigration department sponsored" research, the following kinds of conclusions emerged:

> One third of respondents agreed it was important to "keep out people who are different from most Canadians," while nearly half were "really worried that they may become a minority if immigration is unchecked." (Harper 1992:A24)

Citing a "significant growth in intolerance," this study concluded that previous trends towards growing racial tolerance had reversed. Finally, the study reported that it was no longer the case that the strongest support for immigration is in cities with the most firsthand experience. Instead, it is concluded that in cities with large, immigrant populations it is more likely that "familiarity breeds contempt" (Harper 1992:A24).

Many analysts have argued that growing intolerance during economically troubled times may be tied to the belief that immigrants and refugees are stealing jobs and opportunities from struggling, unemployed Canadians who, but for the immigrant, might otherwise be gainfully employed. Analyst George Frajkor of the Canadian Ethnocultural Council goes so far as to say that:

> the real reason for opposition to immigration may be that people "are afraid of being swamped by strange foreigners, and an economic reason sounds much more acceptable than a racist one." (in Wood 1993:27)

We can only speculate as to whether or not the economic reason is really a cover for racism. But what can be argued with confidence is that there is little evidence to support accusations that immigrants are an economic threat to Canadians. There is, for example, much evidence from the Economic Council of Canada (1991a, 1991b) that could have been used by the Conservative government to try to diffuse some of this growing intolerance. This evidence highlights how the vast majority of immigrants positively contribute to Canadian society. It dispels some of the myths which suggest that most immigrants and refugees to Canada are here only to abuse the social system and take advantage of Canada's generosity.[2] Those cases are most certainly in the minority. In fact, data from the

1986 census show that "contrary to popular belief, the proportion of welfare recipients among recent immigrants (12.5%) is smaller than among the native-born (13.8%)" (Economic Council of Canada 1991a:22; see also de Silva 1992:19).

Nonetheless, rather than trying to diffuse the hostility, Valcourt seems to be exacerbating it (see for example, Finestone in Canada 1992:12551-52). In trying to sell Bill C-86 to Canadians, Valcourt plays on their insecurities by socially constructing the immigrant or refugee as a potential system abuser of whom we should be wary (i.e., guilty until proven innocent). This negativity is further reinforced when Valcourt, on June 16, 1992, at a press conference unveiling the legislation, makes the following statement: "Canadians are compassionate and humane, but we don't want to be taken for a ride" (*Toronto Star* 1992a:A1).[3] Later describing the press conference, MP Rey Pagtakhan (Liberal/Winnipeg North) says the Minister's message has "a distinctly unpleasant after-taste." Pagtakhan continues:

> I felt that in many ways the minister perpetuated myths that the government should be trying to refute, myths that our immigrants and refugees are a strain on the system, that they are a commodity to be managed, that they are accepted or rejected as mere commodities. (Canada 1992:12566)

One of Bill C-86's sharpest critics was the president of the Canadian Labour Congress, Bob White. Two days after Valcourt introduced Bill C-86 in the House of Commons, White attacked the Bill, arguing that "this legislation exposes, once again, the Conservative Government agenda of blaming the victims for the economic woes of this country" (*Toronto Star* 1992b:A3). As George Frajkor of the Canadian Ethnocultural Council notes: "Rather than trying to convince people that their fears about foreigners are groundless, politicians are playing on those fears" (in Wood 1993:26).

Selling Bill C-86

According to Valcourt, the purpose of Bill C-86 is to "provide the *management tools* needed to maintain a *fair, balanced and effective immigration program*" (Immigration Canada 1993:1, emphasis added). Managing immigration requires revisions to three basic immigration programming areas: (1) the management of the immigration movement; (2) the refugee status determination system; and (3) control and enforcement (Valcourt in LEI 25:4). What was the outcome of revising these three major programming areas? Very generally, the Conservative government's idea of managing immigration includes: telling immigrants where they must live in Canada (determined by where in the country their skills are most needed); eliminating the first stage in the refugee determination process (thereby reducing the time necessary to adjudicate the cases of claimants); fingerprinting virtually all refugee claimants (in order to prevent welfare fraud and abuse of the system); barring refugee claimants who enter Canada from "safe"[4] countries; and setting up three different "streams" of entry for people applying for admission to Canada (*Toronto Star* 1992a:A1).

When introduced, Valcourt presented Bill C-86 as the answer for "Managing Immigration" in the 1990s. And it is this idea of managing immigration upon which I will focus. The logic of sanitary coding, particularly the technique of equivocation, is easily applicable to the phrase "managing immigration." Drawing parallels between the phrases "managing immigration" and "controlling immigration" (Dummett 1973: 185), I would argue that managing immigration is a purposively vague and misleading phrase expressly designed to be confusing in its meaning, purpose or intent. As an equivocal term, managing, can have both public and private connotations. According to Reeves:

> The coexistence of public and private connotations, one announcing what ought to be mentioned, the other announcing what ought not to be mentioned, can be regarded as a kind of *code or cipher*. The underlying private message however, is not secret in the sense that it is known only to a select few: most or all of the audience might recognize its presence and be able to decipher it with ease. *It is secret in the sense that the speaker is in a position to refute it.* (1983:193, emphasis added).

With this in mind, consider the term "managing" more closely. Publicly, it takes on a benevolent tone, which implies taking care of Canadians, taking care of immigrants, thereby protecting the image of the Conservative government as a government with humanitarian values. Simultaneously, however, the private, coded meaning of managing is far less altruistic. Does managing, as critics have argued, imply controlling the immigration of people of colour? It is when the politician is challenged to account for his/her remarks that equivocation becomes crucial. Reeves notes that

> the speaker may defend himself [sic] by denying the underlying message, and asserting that the public meaning should be taken at its face value. What he [sic] *really* said is there in public for all to see, and the private connotation is a product of his audience's minds, of their subjective connotations. And how can he [sic] be held responsible for others' subjective interpretations? (1983:193, emphasis added).

From the standpoint of the government, there is an advantage to using equivocation in relation to the law. Ambiguity allows legislators to avoid commitment to any one constituency but it also leaves the legislation open to manipulation by legislators when it seems to be a politically feasible thing to do. Thus, when challenged to explain the phrase "managing," the government attempts to protect itself by giving different responses to varied interest groups. To defend itself against accusations of racism for instance, the Conservative government could argue emphatically that there is no mention of "race" and therefore no violation of the Charter of Rights and Freedoms on this score.[5] When attacked from the other side by racists who say that Bill C-86 doesn't go far enough, Conservatives could argue that managing immigration can be taken to mean controlling the immigration of people of colour. It is simply a more subtle, politically correct way to approach the problem in the current climate.

This is what makes sanitary coding and equivocation so insidious—the "real" intentions of the politician cannot be unquestionably established (Reeves 1983:204). This point notwithstanding, the remarks on Bill C-86 thus far provide ample evidence for suggesting that one purpose of Bill C-86 was to better control the influx of new, visibly different immigrants in order to placate an electorate that was disillusioned with its government, economically vulnerable and increasingly intolerant of immigrants of colour.

How then, does the Conservative government balance the dual demands of appeasing an increasingly xenophobic electorate and protecting Canada's international reputation as a caring and compassionate nation? Towards answering this question, responses to the new management framework will be reviewed from two perspectives: those who support the changes and those who oppose them. I will limit my discussion of the restructuring to two areas—family reunification and the streamlining of the refugee determination process through the "safe" country provision. In doing so, the reader will be provided with a better sense of the duality of law or, put another way, the literal versus the coded meanings that are attached to these amendments.

The Management of the Immigration Movement: Decoding Bill C-86

According to Immigration Canada, the new framework emerging from Bill C-86 will

> establish a new management system that will allow for *clearer, more direct and straightforward control over the immigration program* .... [T]he goal is to achieve and maintain a balance among different immigration objectives that best reflects Canada's needs, and the needs of Canadians. (1992:15, emphasis added).

As the emphasis above suggests, there is one idea in this passage that is particularly striking: that this management framework will bring clarity (i.e., reduce ambiguity) to the immigration process. But will this new framework in practice have such an effect?

Under this system, immigrants are placed into one of three management "streams." In stream one, there is no limit to the number of applicants that can be accepted in any one year. This stream includes immediate family members of people already residing in Canada. Immediate family is defined as a spouse, a fiancé(e) and/or dependent children.[6] Also grouped under stream one are investors,[7] and those people who are classified, by the Immigration and Refugee Board, as Convention refugees[8] (Immigration Canada 1992:16).

Stream two is subject to the limitations set out in the yearly immigration plan. Applications are processed on a "first come, first served" basis. Once quotas have been filled, applications are either: a) no longer accepted; or b) accepted with the understanding that consideration will be deferred until spaces become available in the subsequent year. This stream includes: extended family members of Canadian residents (e.g., parents and grandparents); government-assisted or privately sponsored refugees, those applicants who have "arranged employment, are self-employed or apply to come to Canada as live-in caregivers; and people allowed into Canada under special programs" (ibid.).

Finally, those seeking admission to Canada under stream three would also be subject to limitations established by the annual immigration plan. In this final grouping, independent immigrants[9] are selected solely on the basis of "excellence." Thus, only the best applications in each category—skilled immigrants; those who qualify in designated occupations[10]; and entrepreneurs[11]—will be approved. Once the set number for the given year has been reached, no more applications will be accepted (ibid.).

There have been many critics of this new management framework. According to Canadian Labour Congress President Bob White for example, Bill C-86 "will make Canada less caring, less compassionate, and a less responsible member of the international community. . . . Canada appears to be joining those who would say *Not in my Backyard*" (in Harper 1992:A1). NDP Member of Parliament Margaret Mitchell (Vancouver East) expresses similarly negative sentiments:

> Bill C-86 is not an improvement. It is restrictive, unjust and inhumane in many aspects. First of all, it allows people to buy their way into Canada. That is one of the first priorities. It reflects therefore Conservative and Reform Party values and not the values of fairness and generosity towards immigrants, which have been a Canadian tradition. (Canada 1992:12537).

Critics contend that, under the new legislation, "some immigrants would be more desirable than others and money would talk" (*Toronto Star* 1992a:A1). Valcourt, in general, balks at these kinds of criticisms, arguing that,

> in reality, what we are proposing is that the streams of categories of immigrants recognize that in Canada, family members will be reunited *without limits*, that refugees will be accepted *without limits*, and that

investors will be accepted into Canada *without limits* (Canada 1992:12540, emphasis added).

It is by further exploring this idea of "without limits" that I will shed light on the coded meaning attached to these amendments.

On the Question of Managing Families

The question of family reunification has raised less controversy in relation to Bill C-86 than some of its other elements. However this issue is raised as an example of the way in which a text can be deracialized, but nevertheless have the very subtle effect of controlling the immigration of people of colour. This theme becomes more compelling when the idea of "family," as an equivocal term, is pursued.

Among supporters of the Bill, it is continually reiterated that there will be no limitations on family reunification. Take the following statement by Ross Belsher (Parliamentary Secretary to Minister of Fisheries and Oceans and Minister for the Atlantic Canada Opportunities Agency) as an example:

> One asks if the family reunification plan is alive and well. You bet your boots it is. It is alive and well and we encourage it. *There are no limitations on that.*

> I want the people who are here and looking forward to having their family members join them to know that there is no cause for them to be alarmed about what is in this legislation. It will if anything help them be. It will help them to do away with some of the clutter that is clogging up the system. (Canada 1992:12557, emphasis added).

This perpetual reference to reunification without limitations is somewhat problematic, particularly among those Canadians who have a less conventional understanding of the term family.

In encouraging unlimited family reunification, the government is specifically referring to immediate or nuclear family members. As Sergio Marchi (Liberal, York West) notes, Bill C-86 neither says anything about nor does anything for the extended family (Canada 1992:12501; see also Canada 1992: Mitchell12538-39; in Karpoff:12560). Grandparents, parents and other more distant relatives are, in a sense, reduced to "less than family" status by being processed in lower priority streams that are subject to annual quotas. In her critique of the government plan, MP Shirley Maheu (Liberal/Saint Laurent–Cartierville) sensitizes us to the problem of ethnocentrism that plagues the government's definition:

> We must make sure that family reunification is swift and that it is

sensitive to the various definitions of the family. It should not be one only based on the North American notion, but one that recognizes that *the definition of the family is as varied as the quilt that makes up Canadian society.* (Canada 1992:12529, emphasis added)

Defining the family in a way that better represents the diversity of the Canadian population is further pursued by the Canadian Ethnocultural Council (CEC).

The CEC is "a non-profit, non-partisan coalition of 37 ethnocultural organizations that in turn represent 2000 provincial and local organizations across Canada" (Dick in House of Commons 1992(4):26). The CEC, as an advocate of multiculturalism in Canada, strives to secure "equality of opportunity, rights and dignity for ethnocultural minorities and all other Canadians" (ibid.). From this standpoint, it is not surprising that the CEC has reservations about many aspects of Bill C-86. Most generally, the CEC is concerned about the ways in which the new immigration policy concentrates on Canada's economic needs, while undermining its social needs—i.e., family reunification (House of Commons 1992 (4):32). Consider the following critique by CEC chairperson, Lilian To:

> Although CEC welcomes the proposed amendment that will speed up the reunification of spouses, fiances, and children under the age of 19, we are very concerned that there are much stricter proposals about family reunification. Under the proposed regulation, whereas dependents and spouses are to be placed in the first stream and children under 19 are to be placed in the first stream, without a restriction on numbers, parents and grandparents are to placed in the second stream, where quotas will be in place. *This arbitrary division fails to take into account that many cultures have a view of the family unit that is less restrictive and more inclusive than the western one and that includes parents and grandparents as immediate and integral family members* . . . . The critical question that must be dealt with is how important the family and the extended family are to Canadians. . . . (House of Commons 1992(4):29, emphasis added).

Another organization that is disturbed by the tone of Bill C-86 is the National Organization of Immigrant and Visible Minority Women of Canada (NOIVMW). With advocacy as its main activity, NOIVMW presented its views on the Bill "from an immigrant and visible minority women's perspective" (House of Commons 1992(5):5). Miriam Avalos (Board Member, Immigrant and Visible Minority Women Against Abuse) spoke on the question of family immigration by problematizing the Conservative government's definition of a family:

We are very glad about the amendments that spell out the family reunification commitments. At the same time, they do not recognize extended family as part of the family, a concept in many of the countries of the immigrants. The diversity that we have is not really recognized, so in terms of defining the concept we have to take into account that within our cultures we recognize that it is our responsibility not just to help our children, but to help our grandparents. That comes from the background that in many countries there are no such benefits as pensions, old age security and all those kinds of things we are lucky to have in Canada. In those countries the children have to support not just their grandparents but also parents who are not able to work anymore. That has to be taken into account when we define what a family is. It has an impact when people move to Canada and are not able to sponsor the other members they consider their responsibility to support. (House of Commons 1992(5):9)

Finally, consider the remarks of Amy Go, National President of the Chinese Canadian National Council [CCNC]:

Not only in the Chinese Canadian Community, but also in many minority cultural communities, the whole concept of family goes beyond the nuclear family. . . .
I still live with an extended family and I enjoy that kind of family support. It is important to me as it is important to my family members. It is important to the community and the whole society to look at the long term social cost we might incur as a result of separation of families. (House of Commons 1992(8):99-100)

Thematically, there are many parallels among the statements by the CEC, NOIVMW and CCNC. In essence, the message is that, in our multicultural nation, there is little recognition of, or tolerance for, diversified conceptions of the family. Consistent with the trend that Canadians are becoming less accepting of those who cannot become "more like Canadians," the government adopts a normative definition of the family as a management tool. In doing so, only unlimited *nuclear* family reunification is promoted, thereby placating those increasingly intolerant members of the electorate who favour assimilation over the preservation of cultural distinctiveness.

Family reunification has always been a cornerstone of Canadian immigration. It facilitates the process of adaptation to life in Canada—economically, socially and emotionally—and it increases the likelihood that such a process will be successful. History demonstrates that relatives in immigrant families help one another, and it is this supportive setting that causes an immigrant to be a lot more at ease with himself or herself. Even though family reunification enhances the possibility for successful adaptation to life in Canada, the number of family-class immigrants has dropped from 49.6 percent of all landings in 1984 to only 40 percent of all landings in 1992 (To in House of Commons 1992(4):30).

Beyond reuniting families, this new management framework gives the government more power and control over the kinds of new immigrant families that will gain admission to Canada. More crudely stated, the possibility of weeding out "the undesirables" is greater under the new system. Consider the following elaboration.

In order to reunite a family in Canada, someone must first come as an independent immigrant and then apply to bring his/her family to Canada under stream one.[12] Thus, if a person applies under the independent stream number three, how will s/he be evaluated? According to the new management framework, pools will be created and only the best from within each pool will be chosen. Choosing immigrants on the basis of excellence, in and of itself, is not problematic. But what is problematic is deciding how excellence or the best will be defined, and who will have the power to make such a determination. Additionally, how does one guarantee that the selection of criteria for excellence will not systematically exclude/restrict immigration from particular countries or parts of the world? In debate on this question, MP Warren Allmand (Liberal/Notre-Dame-de-Grace, Quebec) outlines this potential scenario very well:

> Some people look at this [amendment] as first of all an attempt to justify giving more control to the government, and then the government having the ability to choose, as you say, the best from the pools, to refuse applications, to refuse visas and keep picking the best as a means of. . . . One might ask how this corresponds to the provisions in the bill that there should be no discrimination in our immigration policy.
>
> One can see a government building up its own constituency by favouring immigrants who feed its stream of support—I'm putting it in very callous terms—when you can pick and choose among classes. You decide you are going to require a certain type of immigrant based on what you call excellence, so that you don't need anymore applications from India perhaps, or from Latin America, or from Africa, but you need more applications from Yugoslavia or Europe. When I say Yugoslavia, it could be any country. Or you choose more entrepreneurs, and fewer unskilled.
>
> We saw what was just done with respect to domestic workers where the government has virtually cut off domestic workers from the Caribbean by insisting on grade 12 and a six month training program. It says that is so we can get excellence, but in fact what it does is end

up restricting immigrants from one part of the world. (House of Commons 1992(3):15-16)

The point to be emphasized here, once again, is that excellence is an equivocal term. In a pluralist society, it may connote different things to different people. Thus, while Conservatives may argue that the standard of excellence is established on the basis of an objective points system, there is still room for discretion[13] as immigration officials must decide who among the pool is the best.

The authority granted to the government by this Bill will give it the power to tilt the immigration movement back towards Europe and the United States, *should it so choose*. After all, as Allmand notes, "it hasn't been unknown for governments to do things to support their own interests in the past, once they've been given the authority" (House of Commons 1992(3):20). It remains to be seen what kind of immigrants the government's criteria for excellence will bring to Canada, and how these immigrants will impact upon the Canadian family of the future.

Managing Refugees and the Safe Country Provision

In the discussion thus far, it has been noted that the theme of Bill C-86 is "Managing Immigration." While immigration management and refugee determination and protection are really two separate matters, Bill C-86 tries to merge the two. According to David Matas (President of the Canadian Council of Refugees), this amalgamation creates serious problems for refugees. Matas contends that

> the bill itself really does not approach the refugee issue from the angle of refugee protection. . . .
>
> Really, immigration management and refugee protection are two different things and require two different approaches. Immigrants are people who are coming to Canada to settle permanently. Refugees are people being forced to flee a situation of danger, often on a moment's notice. Management suggests that Canada is choosing its immigrants in a planned way. Yet refugees in fact in law and by terms of Canada's international obligations are self-selected.
>
> *Managing immigration really means, in a refugee protection context, denying protection to people who otherwise might be allowed and entitled to come as refugees.* That is indeed the effect of many of the provisions in the bill. They make it more difficult for refugees to seek protection or even to arrive to Canada to make a claim for protection. (House of Commons 1992(5):37, emphasis added)

From a practical standpoint, Bill C-86 is more concerned with controlling the influx of refugees to Canada than it is with protecting refugees. Humanitarian concerns are downplayed, and refugees become simply another category of immigrants to be managed within the new immigration streams. Given the above, this section will explore one way that this particular category of immigrants can be managed—through the use of the "Safe Country Provision." Consistent with the argument thus far, the Safe Country Provision is depicted as little more than code for "controlling the immigration of people of colour." Having set the tone for the argument to follow, it is necessary to first review those dimensions of Canada's refugee determination process that are relevant to the current Safe Country Provision in Bill C-86.

Canada's refugee determination process in context
In the explanatory material released with Bill C-86, Immigration Canada began by contextualizing the changes to the immigration process. First and foremost, in order to justify the need to better control or manage immigration, it was necessary to convince Canadians that immigration had somehow become unmanageable. Hence, the many references to "growing, unpredictable, large scale movements of people" (1992:3). We can easily envision foreigners flooding our gates when we read passages like the following: "Some estimates suggest that today, as many as eighty million people—more than three times the entire population of Canada—are moving from one country to another at any given time" (Immigration Canada 1992:4). Specifically on the question of refugees:

> Millions of these people are fleeing persecution, civil strife or economic deprivation in their home countries. . . . [t]he number of people claiming refugee status and seeking protection continues to grow. In 1983, 95 000 people sought asylum in Organization for Economic Development (OECD) Countries. In 1991, the number was 700,000—an increase of almost 800%. (Immigration Canada 1992:4)

To create further unease, we are told that not only is the number of people claiming refugee status rising sharply, "the proportion of claimants who are found to be genuine refugees is falling" (Immigration Canada 1992:4). By setting the stage in this way, it is easy for one to construct an image of our borders being inundated by foreigners who are less than genuine.

Through such statements, the government appears to be trying to construct a negative image of the immigration and refugee process in Canada in order to justify the need for greater management of the operation. Particularly in the case of refugees, we get a false sense that we are being overwhelmed with people because our "too liberal" refugee policy attracts "more than Canada's share of refugees" (Refugee Lawyers Association in House of Commons 1992(5):5A-27). In reality, the situation is quite different. According to evidence from the

Centre for Refugee Studies:

> Canada receives fewer refugee claimants per capita than other coun-
> tries in the western world, and much fewer than many developing
> countries such as Iran and Kenya. . . . On average Western nations
> receive 1 refugee claimant per 850 residents. Canada receives signifi-
> cantly less than average at 1 refugee claimant per 1000 residents.
> Germany, by comparison, receives 1 claimant for each 250 residents.
> (House of Commons 1992(5):5A-27)

Having created this scenario, Immigration Canada stresses the need to develop a system that will more efficiently deal with refugees—a system that will be better able to manage the number and types of people who gain entry into Canada through the refugee determination process. Under a more efficient, streamlined system, it is argued, processing times for claims will be reduced significantly and those genuinely in need will better be served.

Refugee determination: before and after Bill C-86

Before Bill C-86, refugee determination included a two-hearing process. The first hearing was designed to establish the credibility of the claimant—that is, "whether the claimant is eligible to have the claim determined and if so, whether the claim has a credible basis" (Young 1992:2). This decision is based on the deliberations of two people, an adjudicator and one member of the Refugee Division of Immigration. The hearing is very formal and the claimant is guaranteed legal council at the hearing. If the claimant cannot afford his/her own council, it will provided by the minister, at the minister's expense (ibid.).

Although initially implemented in 1989 to screen for system abusers, this first hearing proved to be unduly complicated and costly. From the perspective of the Conservative government, there was no justification for a first hearing since "some 94% of the claimants have been found to have credible claims" (ibid.). Thus, one way to streamline the refugee determination process was to eliminate the first hearing, which would include elimination of government-funded council for the claimant. In lieu of the first hearing, a claimant would be referred to a senior immigration officer (SIO) who would then assess eligibility (3).

Many critics of Bill C-86 have strongly opposed this move by the government, that, in essence, awards more discretionary power to the SIO. In defence of its actions, the Ministry of Immigration argued that there would be no room for discretion by the SIO in the determination of eligibility. It would be strictly an administrative decision based on a checklist. In the words of Peter Harder (Associate Deputy Minister, Immigration), "the SIO is dealing with facts as opposed to matters of judgement" (House of Commons 1992(3):88). What then would be included on this checklist? According to the provisions of Bill C-86, a SIO could deny claimants access to the refugee determination system on the basis that they are *not eligible* if they:

    a)   have been recognized as a Convention refugee by another country, to which they can be returned;

    b)   *came to Canada, directly or indirectly, from a country (other than their country of nationality or habitual residence) that has been prescribed by the Governor in Council as a country that complies with Article 33 of the Convention*[14] *(that is a country does not return people directly or indirectly to the frontiers of countries where they fear persecution on the named grounds)*;

    c)   are making a repeat claim without having been out of Canada for 90 days;

    d)   have already been determined in Canada or by a visa officer abroad to be a Convention refugee; or

    e)   have been determined by an adjudicator in an inquiry to be security risks, serious criminals, or war criminals, and the Minister certifies that they are a danger to the public in Canada or that it is not in the public interest to hear the claim. (Young 1995a:4-5, emphasis added)

Arguably, a number of these criteria could be subject to interpretation or, to use Harder's words, "matters of judgement." At present, however, only criterion (b) mentioned above, the Safe Country Provision, will be analyzed. This choice is a deliberate one. Specifically, it is my contention that the text of this provision has been deracialized and *appears* to be non-discriminatory. In reality however, the application of this provision would result in controlling the immigration of people of colour.

The safe country concept
The notion of "safe country" did not emerge with Bill C-86. In fact, it was a very controversial aspect of Bill C-55. This latter piece of legislation, which received Royal Assent on July 21, 1988, "radically altered the procedures for determining claims to Convention refugee status made within Canada" (Young 1991b:1). Theoretically under Bill C-55, the claimant could be rendered ineligible under a Safe Country Provision. However, when Bill C-55 came into force, no "safe country" list had been provided by the Governor in Council. Because there was no list, the Safe Country Provision did not come into effect with the Bill (Young 1991b:5).

    The initial purpose of introducing the Safe Country Provision was to prevent "asylum shopping"—that is, "coming to Canada from a position of safety as a matter of personal choice" (Young 1991b:12). Essentially, it was to remind the world that Canada is not the only country that has an obligation to protect refugees; therefore, Canada should be required to assist only those who have no other safe haven. There was, however, a fundamental problem with trying to make such a provision operational. As Young (1991b:13-14) notes: "in international law, there is nothing to compel any of the countries on any list that Cabinet might prescribe to accept the return of most claimants, absent their agreement to do so" (see also Matas in House of Commons 1992(5):38). Given this legal complication, Canada maintains an interest in establishing such agreements with other countries. In fact, on amending this provision for inclusion in Bill C-86, the question of agreements became a factor.

> In prescribing the list of countries to which people may be returned, the law directs the Governor in Council to take into account four factors: a) whether the country was party to the Convention [Relating to the Status of Refugees]; b) the country's policies and practices with respect to Convention refugee claims; c) the country's record with respect to human rights; and [the following new criterion] d) whether the country is party to an agreement with Canada for such returns.[15] (Young 1995a:17)

Under the Safe Country Provision of Bill C-86, refugee claimants could be rendered ineligible if they travelled to Canada directly *or* indirectly from a prescribed country. Under Bill C-86, assessment of eligibility on the basis of this criterion does not allow for any consideration of how the claimant might be treated if returned to a prescribed country. Instead the only relevant question for the SIO is whether the claimant came "from or through" a prescribed country. If the answer to this question is yes, the claimant is rendered ineligible (Young 1992:31).

From the perspective of the government's immigration officials, this provision would minimize the use of discretion on the part of the SIO. Supposedly, rendering a decision of ineligibility by reference to a Safe Country Provision would simplify the process. However, there are many problems associated with the concept of a safe country list. Much of this is related to ministerial discretion. Beyond compliance with Article 33 of the Convention (which is mandatory), the minister uses discretion when deciding: how other criteria for assessing safety will be interpreted; what considerations, beyond safety criteria, will affect a country's chances for inclusion on the list; and with whom to consult in the construction of such a list.[16] To more clearly illustrate the potential problems with this provision, consider the case of the United States as a prescribed country.

Given that some 49 percent of refugee claimants arrive in Canada via the U.S. (Young 1991b:16), it would be very much in the interests of Canada to work out a "border-sharing arrangement" (Young 1992:6) with the U.S. on the question of refugee determination. There are obvious political and diplomatic reasons for placing the U.S. on a safe country list. It would also expedite considerably Canada's refugee determination process. The problem arises when we are forced to acknowledge that historically, the U.S.'s treatment of refugees has been less than admirable. As Warren Allmand (House of Commons 1992(8):74) notes, the U.S. has consistently been more accepting of refugees fleeing from countries where there is a leftist government in power (e.g., Cuba) and less tolerant of refugees fleeing from a country where the regime in power "has some sort of working relationship with the Government of the United States" (e.g., El Salvador, Guatemala). Evidence from American lawyer Arthur Helton corroborates this point:

> Traditionally, the United States has, in its asylum adjudication activities, reflected its role as one of the primary combatants in the Cold War. In that sense, since the enactment of the *Refugee Act* of 1980, one could look at approval levels in the asylum system ... of about 25% and then identify a number of nationalities that were disproportionately and differentially treated poorly, such as Haitians, Guatemalans, and Salvadorans who experienced approval levels of 1-3%. Others, eastern Europeans, then Soviet nationals, experienced approval levels anywhere from 50-80% .... [S]ome refugees were considered as trophies and other as embarrassments in this fierce ideological struggle. (House of Commons 1992(8):74)

What this discussion suggests is that, contrary to what the government would have us believe, the situation around safe countries is not a simple one, nor are the responsibilities of the SIO so clear cut. Not considering how the claimant might be treated upon return to a prescribed country can have serious personal and legal ramifications.

> It should be remembered that the Convention prevents the return in any matter whatsoever to the frontiers of a country where a person fears persecution. Thus, unless an agreement with a listed country specifically provided that a returned person would be allowed to stay or that the person's claim would be heard on its merits, and the person would not merely be sent elsewhere, the claimant's security could be threatened. Since agreements with Canada are not a precondition to placing a country on the list, sending claimants to countries without agreements could be even more problematic. Such threats to claimant's life and security of person, it will no doubt be argued, would violate both the Convention and the Charter. (Young 1992:31-32)

Having introduced this complex and controversial provision, I can now return to the question most pertinent to the theme of this chapter—how would the Safe

Country Provision, which makes no mention of "race," allow the government to control the immigration of people of colour?

Deciphering the safe country concept

> A person who claims to be a Convention Refugee is not eligible to have the claim heard by the Refugee division if the person . . . comes to Canada, directly or indirectly, from a country, other than a country of the person's nationality, or where the person has no country of nationality, the country of the person's habitual residence, that is a prescribed country . . . . (Bill C-86, Section 46.01(1)(b))

According to Patricia Wong (Executive Member, Refugee Lawyers Association), one of the many reasons that the Refugee Lawyers Association is opposed to the Safe Country Provision is because it discriminates against people of the developing world (in House of Commons 1992(5):61). Consistent with Wong's contention, the essence of the argument to follow is that the Safe Country Provision, when operational, would systematically exclude those refugee populations from the developing world (most of whom are visibly different) who cannot get direct flights out of unsafe countries.

This particular provision of Bill C-86 is reminiscent of the discriminatory legislation passed by the Canadian government in 1908 to restrict the entry of East Indian immigrants into Canada. As outlined in Chapter 1, the *Continuous Journey Stipulation* allowed refusal of entry to immigrants who came to Canada "otherwise than by continuous journey from the countries of which they were natives or citizens, and upon through tickets purchased in that country" (Bolaria and Li 1988:170). The *Continuous Journey Stipulation* bears striking resemblance to the Safe Country Provision of Bill C-86 (for further discussion, see House of Commons 1992(4):64-65, 73-76). As the Inter-Church Committee for Refugees suggests, historians correctly criticized the *Continuous Journey Stipulation* because it was used as a means of controlling what groups of people would be permitted to stay in Canada. They further contend that, on reflection, many historians will offer a similar criticism of the Safe Country Provision (4A-58, 65).

It is important to recognize a number of points here. First, it is estimated that approximately 95 percent of the world's refugees are in developing countries (4A-59). Second, the majority of refugee claimants in Canada, given the previous statistic, are unable to come to Canada without passing through another country (4A-58). As the Canadian Labour Congress (CLC) notes in its brief to the House, "because of our geographic location relative to the refugee source countries and because of international travel arrangements, most refugees will land or pass through the United States or Europe" (House of Commons 1992(8):8A-9). Consistent with the position of the Refugee Lawyer's Association, the CLC contends that the Safe Country Provision clearly supports only those refugees that have the financial means to fly directly from their country of origin (ibid.). Given the above, how, in more tangible terms, would the Safe Country Provision impact upon the refugee's ability to gain access to the Canadian system? The Jesuit Centre for Social Faith and Justice offers the following hypothetical analysis, had the provision been operational in 1991:

> If these changes had been in effect in . . . 1991, the following situation could have resulted. In all there were 30,539 claims made in 1991. Of these, 19,111 were made at border points, with the balance being made by people who were already in Canada. Looking then, at the 19,111 claims made at border points, 14,780 were made by people who came through safe third countries, that is, the United States, European countries and Japan. All are countries which would no doubt end up on the list of prescribed countries. If all of these 14,780 border claimants had been ruled ineligible, then 48% fewer claimants would have been heard by the CRDD [Convention Refugee Determination Division]. (House of Commons 1992(10):10A-27)

The ultimate effect of the legislation then, without ever mentioning the word "race," is to control a particular dimension of the refugee population— developing world refugees, the majority of whom are classified by the government as visible minorities. It is this idea of controlling the immigration of people of colour that Christine Kurata (Executive Member, Refugee Lawyers Committee) pursues in her presentation to the Legislative Committee on Bill C-86:

> Without a doubt and I'd like to be very direct with the committee—we, [the Refugee Lawyers Association], feel that this provision discriminates against black, brown and yellow people, against people from the developing world. The bottom line of this provision is that most people who can get to Canada on connecting flights[17] are people who are coming from European countries. If you come from Asia or from Africa or from South America or Central America, you simply cannot do that. We presume that there will be a discussion among airlines and different enforcement agencies that will ensure that if flights aren't routed now, they will be routed 100% through countries that will be on the prescribed list.
>
> We're very concerned for many reasons. . . . [W]hen you look at the statistics of the Immigration and Refugee Board, you'll see that since 1989, the majority of people who have received protection have been from developing world countries, mainly from Somalia and Sri Lanka. . . . This bill is being considered precisely at a time when the

situation for such people is most desperate. (House of Commons 1992(5):71)

After making her opening remarks, Kurata concretizes her discussion of discrimination by using as an example the differential treatment of refugees from the former Yugoslavia and Somalia. Consider the following exchange between the chair of the legislative committee and Kurata.

Ms. Kurata: For example, today we discussed the announcement that was made. I have not seen the press release, but I understand Mr. Valcourt announced today that the entrance of 26,000 refugees, I believe, from Yugoslavia would be facilitated. We applaud that. We feel that's a desperate situation and people should be helped. But we do not understand why it is in the Horn of Africa in situations like this where, quite frankly, many, many more people are being killed, many more civilians, the possibility of some sort of solution is, quite frankly, impossible, completely remote. We do not understand why people in those situations are not being helped. We ask the committee to please consider how this is going to affect other generations in a country that is a multicultural country. As we know, there have been situations in the past where we feel we failed other people. We failed, for example, the Jews who were—

The Chairman: Ms. Kurata, I believe you are making a very fine statement and have things absolutely correct insofar as it goes, for sure. We are under a very short timeframe and I really want to ask some other members to put their questions to you on this bill itself.

Ms. Kurata: Yes

The Chairman: I listened to the minister's press conference this morning too. He did point out that with respect to Somalia, there were some 11,600 Somalians in Canada and more going to come obviously. That is more of a general policy.

Ms. Kurata: But, sir, this section will stop precisely that group of people from making plans.

The Chairman: You are making that point very well and we will certainly follow up with that in the Bill. Mr. Reid, would you put your questions. (House of Commons 1992(5):71—72)

There are a number of interesting dimensions to this exchange. The most obvious one is the way in which the chair clearly cuts off Kurata, acknowledging, albeit not confronting, the issues that she is presenting. During the exchange, when the chair tries to defend Valcourt's position on Somalia, Kurata is quick to point out how the Safe Country Provision that Valcourt has adopted will prevent any further consideration of Somalian refugee claimants. Upon reminding the chair of the coded meaning of the Safe Country Provision, he very quickly acknowledges the point and moves on to another speaker to prevent further discussion of the issue.

The Safe Country Provision represents a classic example of ideological deracialization. By using the logic of sanitary coding and the technique of equivocation, legislators have created a clause that is ambiguous as to its meaning or true intent. This ambiguity allows politicians to address, yet remain non-committal to, the diverse concerns arising out its various constituencies. For example, it is possible that the Safe Country Provision will be challenged on constitutional grounds. Specifically, does the provision discriminate on the basis of "race" or nationality, which would be in direct violation of Section 15 of the Canadian *Charter of Rights and Freedoms*? In response, defenders of the provision could argue that there is absolutely no mention of "race" or nationality and hence no violation of the *Charter*. Rather, in an effort to keep out system abusers, the government is simply trying to manage more efficiently the number and types of people who gain entry into Canada through the refugee determination process. But could there be an underlying message? What is the private intent of the Safe Country Provision? Is it to control the immigration of people of colour? It is when the politician is challenged in this way that equivocation becomes essential, for however much the audience may see racism or discrimination in the provision, the politician is always in a position to refute the interpretation.

The effects of the Safe Country Provision remain to be seen. Although enshrined in law, the provision is not operational because no safe country list is currently in place (Young 1995a:4). But even if such a list did exist, "there is nothing in international law to compel the countries on any such list to accept the return of most of these claimants, absent of their agreement to do so" (Young 1995a:16). At present, Canada does not have any formal international agreements but "a draft agreement is under discussion with the United States and the government has announced its intention to seek an agreement with certain European governments" (ibid.).

Conclusion

The purpose of this chapter has been to explore the process through which laws are constructed, underscoring all the while that the content of laws changes in response to the historically specific experiences of individuals. As the chapter unfolded, it became increasingly apparent that, while laws could be socially constructed as mutually beneficial to the concerned parties, these purported gains or benefits often serve to do little more than reinforce already-existing forms of systemic discrimination.

In analyzing Bill C-86, I noted that the nature of immigration legislation at any given historical moment is very much shaped by the economic climate at the time. I also stressed the duality of law—i.e., the literal versus the coded intentions of the legislation. However, towards better appreciating the persistence of racial discrimination within immigration, I did not conceptualize the problem as one of contradictions between ideology and practice. Instead, as with the *Live-In Caregiver Program*, the interplay between the text of law and law talk was explored, highlighting, in particular, how the logic of sanitary coding and the technique of equivocation allow privately racist ideas to be communicated through language that is publicly defensible as non-racist.

Notes

1. For example, the number of immigrants and refugees who have gained admission to Canada has increased from 88,000 in 1983 to 250,000 at present (Valcourt in Canada 1992:12540).
2. For a discussion of "the fine line between myth and reality," see Marchi in Canada 1992:12500.
3. This social construction of the immigrant as "system abuser" is later bolstered by Prime Minister Kim Campbell, when in June of 1993, she announces that "all immigration operations in Canada and abroad, as well as business immigration and refugees," will be handled by the newly created "Public Security" department (Immigration Canada 1993:1).
4. I will come back to a consideration of the potential problems that come with the "safe" country provision of the Bill.
5. Interestingly, Valcourt provides just such a response when he is accused by critics of "playing to the right" and attempting to reach the same constituency as the Reform Party. The Reform Party has repeatedly been accused of racism for its attacks on the immigration system. Although one can easily draw parallels between the philosophies of the Reform and Conservative Parties on the question of immigration, Valcourt categorically denies any similarity—"There's nothing, but absolutely nothing in C-86 that closely resembles the coded message of Preston Manning regarding Immigration"(Valcourt in Thompson 1993:B7; see also Caragata in *Toronto Star* 1992).
6. Dependent children, including adopted children, are those who are: unmarried, and nineteen years of age or under; those who are full-time students; and those who are mentally or physically challenged and unable to support themselves (Immigration Canada 1993:35).
7. An investor, according to Immigration Canada (1993:36) is:
    a person who has a proven track record and who has an accumulated net worth of at least $500,000 and who makes an investment as required in a project which has been assessed by the province as being of significant benefit to its economy and which will contribute to the creation or continuation of employment opportunities for Canadian citizens and permanent residents.
8. A Convention refugee is any person who:

a) by reason of a well-founded fear of persecution for reasons of race, religion, nationality, membership in a particular social group or political opinion: i) is outside the country of his (sic) nationality, and is unable or, by reason of that fear, is unwilling to avail himself of protection of that country or ii) not having a country of nationality, is outside the country of his former habitual residence and is unable or, by reason of that fear, is unwilling to return to that country; and b) has not ceased to be a Convention refugee by such reason as voluntary repatriation (Immigration Canada 1993:34).

9. Distant family members, who do not qualify under stream one or stream two, will be classed as independents, sometimes in designated occupations or as entrepreneurs (Robitaille in Canada 1992:12565).

10. A designated occupation is "an occupation in a locality or area in Canada designated by the Minister, after consultation with the relevant provincial authority, as a locality or area in which workers in that occupation are in short supply" (Immigration Canada 1993:35).

11. An entrepreneur is:

an immigrant who intends and has the ability to establish, purchase or make a substantial investment in a business or commercial venture in Canada that will: make a significant contribution to the economy; and create or continue employment opportunities in Canada for one or more Canadian citizens or permanent residents, other than the entrepreneur and his or her dependents. And who intends and has the ability to provide active and on-going participation in the management of the business or commercial venture (Immigration Canada 1993:35).

12. The obvious exception in this case is the Canadian citizen who sponsors a spouse/ fiance, and/or children who live abroad.

13. The discretionary powers of immigration officers is discussed in some detail in Chapter 1.

14. According to Arthur Helton (Director, Refugee Project, Lawyer's Committee on Human Rights), "non-refoulement" is the basic tenet of refugee law (House of Commons 1992(8):8A-41). This principle stipulates that it is the right of a refugee not to be returned to "a place of prospective persecution." This internationally recognized principle is embodied in Article 33 of the 1951 United Nations *Convention Relating to the Status of Refugees*. Under Article 33, no signatory state, or complying country

shall expel or return a refugee ("refouler") in any manner whatsoever to the frontiers of territories where his [sic] life or freedom would be threatened on account of his race, religion, nationality, membership of a particular social group or political opinion (House of Commons 1992(8):8A-41).

15. Agreements between countries are not legal prerequisites to the placement of countries on a "safe country" list (Young 1995a:17).

16. For a more detailed discussion of the problems associated with a "safe country" list, the reader is referred to Boissin (House of Commons 1992(4):9); Turley (House of Commons 1992(4):65-66); Helton (House of Commons 1992(8):73-74).

17. Reference here is being made to Section 46.01(3)(a) of Bill C-86: " a person who is in a country solely for the purpose of joining a connecting flight to Canada shall not be considered as coming to Canada from that country."

6

Concluding Remarks

For centuries, Canada has been identified as "a nation of immigrants" (Samuel 1990:383). In fact, recent statistics indicate that one out of every six Canadian residents was born outside of Canada (Immigration Canada 1992:9). In some way, direct or indirect, immigration touches the lives of all Canadians. As former Immigration Minister Bernard Valcourt remarked in the preface to his report *Managing Immigration: A Framework for the 1990s*:

> immigration has played a part in shaping the shared values that unite us as Canadians, strengthening a fundamental respect for diversity and human rights that has been part of Canada from the beginning. And throughout our history, immigration has helped us to build a thriving and competitive economy. . . . Immigrants have come to Canada from all parts of the world. . . . And they have brought with them a single unifying belief: a belief that Canada is a land of great opportunity.

Valcourt's remarks place immigration in a very positive light. He suggests that immigration is a unifying force for Canadians. It helps us to prosper economically and, through our contact with diverse groups of people, we learn to become more tolerant and respecting of difference. This image, however, does not reflect the reality of all immigrants.

Thematically, this book has explored the process through which racism is manifested in contemporary Canadian immigration law, policies and practices. I began by noting that historically, in relation to Canadian Immigration, substantial gains have been made by visible minority populations. The law, *in principle*, has moved from being restrictive to non-discriminatory. The explicitly restrictive clause of the 1910, 1919 and 1952 *Acts*—38(c)—has been removed. In fact since 1962, there has been a shift towards universal, non-discriminatory treatment of all applicants. This principle of equality is embodied in Section 3(f) of Canada's current *Immigration Act*. This literal gain, in the form of a non-discriminatory clause, has enabled more people of colour to come to Canada. But, regardless of this new wave of immigrants to Canada, the *Immigration Act* is not as just and fair as it appears to be. In subtle ways, immigration law continues to be racist. The question thus becomes: how does one reconcile the contradictions between the ideology and practice of equality?

Towards a reconciliation of the contradictions, this book highlights how law is inescapably *political*. Law-makers recognize that, in the law creation process, competing interests must be addressed. Furthermore, the enshrinement in law of the interests of any particular group is the outcome of complex political

91

negotiations. To facilitate this process of negotiation, symbolic ideals like equity and fairness are embodied in the law, symbols that are so vague and all-embracing that "most members of society can accept or support them in some interpretation" (Cotterrell 1992:103).

I began by tracing the historical transition from explicitly discriminatory to non-discriminatory legislation. What became clear is that, throughout this period of transition, one goal has remained constant—immigration control. The nature of control varies, at times being blatant, at other times being more subtle. The form control takes at any given moment is determined by the way in which law-makers and politicians address three, often competing factors: the desire to populate Canada with British people (or those most like the British); the concerns and demands of the international community; and economic factors (Law Union of Ontario 1981:17).

Initially, law and policy as a means of controlling immigration were racist in orientation, assimilationist in objective. Striving to preserve the British character of the country, law-makers considered immigrants of colour the least desirable, of "lesser stock" than whites and least likely to assimilate. During Canada's nation-building period, when labour needs could not be met with immigrants from preferred source countries, immigrants of colour were admitted to fill the shortage. However, when the work was done and there was a surplus of labour in Canada, the federal government began to pass obviously discriminatory pieces of legislation in an attempt to curtail the undesirable visible minority presence in the country.

Changing demands of the labour market, international pressure for openness within the context of a multiracial Commonwealth (Hawkins 1989:39), and growing internal pressure from increasingly influential minority groups brought an official end to racial discrimination within immigration law and policy. Universal non-discriminatory principles were enshrined, by the state, in Section 3(f) of Canada's *Immigration Act*. Accordingly "race," nationality and ethnicity, as criteria for selecting immigrants, were abandoned, being replaced by the universally applicable, purportedly fair and objective, points system. Yet despite the theoretical commitment to equality, discrimination in less obvious forms persisted. The number and location of immigration offices outside of Canada and the discretion awarded to immigration officers in determining "adaptability" suggested that immigration, to some degree, could still be controlled. But the nature of this control is more complex and subtle.

Developing an appreciation of this complexity necessarily began with a review of ideology as it is related to law and the reconstitution of hegemony. Here, a conceptual framework was created to investigate the role of law in reconstituting and legitimizing unequal social relations in Canada's capitalist, liberal-democratic state. Maintaining that the basis of legitimacy within modern society is the law, I explored how the state strives to fulfil its two, often contradictory functions of accumulation and legitimation (O'Connor 1973:6).

The creation of this conceptual framework reaffirmed that explanations for the differential treatment of immigrants could not be reduced exclusively to economic/class concerns. Specifically, in a multicultural, liberal, capitalist democracy like Canada, the state must accommodate a multiplicity of interests.

Because Canadian society is distinguished by various philosophies, like capitalism, liberal-democracy and multiculturalism, the process of state legitimation is complex. As one of the leading capitalist countries in the world, Canada's economic order is characterized by inequality, coercive and alienating relationships and exploitation. Accordingly, the continual reproduction of unequal social relations becomes central to the persistence and advancement of capitalism. On the other hand, Canada purports to be a liberal-democratic society in which the lives of all Canadians are governed by principles of liberty and equality. These liberal-democratic principles are reaffirmed in Canada's *Multiculturalism Act* (1988). Embodied in the *Act* is a doctrine that "provides a political framework for the official promotion of cultural differences and social equality as an integral component of the social order" (Elliot and Fleras 1992:272). In effect, the *Multiculturalism Act* is designed to be a tool for more effectively and positively managing the growing ethnic and racial diversity in Canada. Because there are contradictions among these philosophies, and competing goals to be met, the state, in its quest for legitimacy, must actively pursue measures that will satisfy a more diversified constituency. With this in mind, a comparison of the processes of ideological racialization and deracialization helps us to better appreciate the historically-specific, subtle form of racism that here emerges.

Ideological racialization, or the increasing use of "race" in discourse, describes the process of individuals using racial categories to account for what they perceive and how they act (Reeves 1983:174). When this process of racial categorization is awarded a negative evaluative component, racism is the result. Ultimately, attributing negative characteristics to particular categories may be used to rationalize and legitimize the exploitation and marginalization of particular elements of the population. While this approach might satisfy the interests of the state's capitalist constituency, it is unlikely to be as favourably received internationally or among the increasingly effectual racial and ethnic communities in Canada. How, then, does the state continue to operate in the interests of capital, preserve its international reputation and sustain support among racial and ethnic voters in Canada? Expressed more generally, how does the government negotiate among the interests of its various constituencies? One solution becomes to engage in a process of ideological deracialization. To avoid accusations of racism, state actors remove from discourse all explicit references to, and evaluations of, racial categories. The effectiveness of this strategy is particularly evident in relation to law.

Law is socially constructed to be a detached, objective and neutral expression of societal values that transcends the immediate interests of the individual.

But law plays a central role in the reproduction and legitimation of unequal social relations. How, then, do laws come to be shaped in and reflective of the interests and experiences of those who participate in the relations of ruling? The answer materialized from the documentary analysis of immigration law and policies.

The exploration of the interplay between the text of law and law talk addressed the question of how racist practices could persist, even in the presence of deracialized, non-discriminatory texts. Noting that the nature of immigration legislation at any given historical moment is very much shaped by the economic climate at the time, two amendments to Canada's *Immigration Act* were investigated. Throughout the critical analysis of the *Live-In Caregiver Program* and Bill C-86, emphasis was placed on how these documents direct individuals to think about and view the world of immigration within predetermined conceptual boundaries that are not disruptive to the ruling order.

Perhaps the most significant part of the documentary analysis is that which deals with the interplay between the text of law and law talk. By providing an alternative interpretation of the documents, the analysis concretely highlights the duality of law. Exposing this duality with counter-hegemonic interpretations of legislative changes reveals how purportedly non-discriminatory legislation can be used to subtly perpetuate social inequality. This section also raises the possibility that the persistence of racial discrimination within immigration is not necessarily a problem of contradictions between ideology and practice. In fact, because equivocation has become institutionalized in both the text of law and law talk, it is virtually impossible to verify the real intentions behind the legislation.

The use of equivocation in law allows legislators to avoid commitment to any one constituency, but it also leaves the legislation open to manipulation when the government must negotiate among the various demands of diversified interest groups. Consider, as examples, the *Live-In Caregiver Program* and Bill C-86. In essence, both amendments represent immigration-controlling measures that are potentially discriminatory towards Blacks and people of colour. However, given the explicit, anti-discrimination clause (Section 3(f)) of the *Immigration Act*, no legislator or politician supporting the changes will openly admit to having any knowledge of the discriminatory potential of the amendments. If indeed there are racist intentions underlying the changes, the use of equivocation makes them very difficult to unquestionably establish. Equivocation then, plays an integral role in the state's quest for legitimacy.

As the research by Simmons and Keohane reveals:

> it can no longer be simply assumed that labour and capital (or their lobbies, in the form of unions and business associations etc.) are the only important actors pressuring the state in the immigration field since the provinces ... and ethnic communities are also involved. (1992:426, 429-30)

Thus to legitimize its social position, the state relies on equivocation as a means for providing different responses to divergent interests. For example, to the various ethnic communities and advocacy groups that might accuse the state of racism, a response might be that there is no mention of "race" and, therefore, no violation of the *Charter of Rights and Freedoms*. On the other hand, among those elements of the electorate that are economically vulnerable and growing increasingly intolerant of visibly different immigrants, the amendments might be presented as mechanisms that will, more subtly, control the immigration of people of colour. What this example suggests is that it is possible to communicate privately racist ideas through discourse that can be publicly defended as not racist.

This book provides one explanation for the manifestation of racism in contemporary Canadian immigration law, policies and practices. There is, however, much work yet to be done. Since the completion of this project, there has been a change from a Conservative to a Liberal government in Canada. New immigration policies that are more reflective of liberal philosophies have emerged and will continue to emerge. For the purposes of comparison, one might investigate the interplay between the text of law and law talk from a Liberal standpoint in order to determine whether racism will be perpetuated in similarly subtle ways.

According to former Liberal Minister of Immigration and Citizenship Sergio Marchi:

> Immigration is about deciding who we are as a nation and who we want to become in the 21st century. We need a clear and practical vision of the kind of nation we want to build. And Canadians need to help shape that vision. It is important—now, more than ever—for all Canadians to engage in an open, honest discussion about immigration and our future. (in Fontana 1994:2).

With this statement in mind, one might explore how Marchi and his policy advisors dealt with the crisis-like situation created by the June 1994 murder of Toronto police constable Todd Baylis.

The accused, Clinton Gayle, is a twenty-five-year-old native of Jamaica. Gayle, who came to Canada as a landed immigrant in 1977, is a ten-time convicted criminal (*London Free Press* 1994). On March 1, 1991, while serving time in a Guelph jail, Gayle was ordered deported. He was arrested by immigration officials at the same jail in June 1992. Subsequently, he was released on a two thousand dollar security bond while immigration officials tried to obtain the travel documents necessary to send Gayle back to Jamaica. But somehow Gayle's file got misplaced in the bureaucratic maze of immigration, and he was never deported. While this clearly is an instance of how the system can fail, what effect did this highly publicized case have on immigration policies? Police demanded government accountability and called for an RCMP round-up of all dangerous offenders (*London Free Press* 1994b). But who would be classified as a dangerous offender? Who would be considered a threat to Canadian society? Will "race" factor into the determination process? Will any one group of immigrants (e.g., Jamaicans) be more prone to deportation?

A joint RCMP–Immigration Canada task force, operating mainly out of Toronto, Vancouver and Montreal was immediately created and, by September of 1995, 497 foreign-born criminals had been deported (McCarthy 1995). Interestingly, when the government released this information, it was "unable to provide figures . . . on the country of destination" (McCarthy 1995). Because of its successes, the government has decided to make permanent the RCMP–Immigration task force to track foreign criminals (Bell 1995).

Undoubtedly, a review of the interrelationship among racism, crime, and immigration law, policies and practices would provide the foundations for an insightful documentary analysis. Such a review might begin with a critical analysis of Bill C-44. Given first reading in the House of Commons on June 17, 1994 and ultimately receiving Royal Assent on June 15, 1995, Bill C-44 amends the *Immigration Act* to "restrict the rights of those convicted of crimes, facilitate enforcement, streamline certain immigration processes and correct technical errors resulting from the previous immigration bill, Bill C-86" (Young 1995b:1). Margaret Young describes the context within which the current bill has emerged:

> In recent months a number of high profile cases involving criminality and immigrants have come to light. Some involved criminals who were permanent residents and had been given a reprieve from deportation by the *Immigration and Refugee Board* (IRB) in circumstances difficult to understand. At the same time, other perceived abuses in the refugee and immigration system had increasingly aroused public opinion. Although not all amendments in the bill are in response to recent events, some are. . . . (Young 1995b:1)

Beyond questions of criminality, the Liberal government, on November 17, 1995, announced a new policy regarding the points system and the rules of entry into Canada. Two of the most controversial changes in the policy, which took effect in February 1996, were as follows: increasing the number of points awarded to independent applicants for fluency in French or English (from fourteen to twenty), and giving immigration officials more discretion in determining "adaptability" to the labour market (from nine to sixteen) (Cox 1995:A7). In critically examining these amendments one might consider whether these changes are a response by the government to growing anti-immigration sentiment in Canada. Will the greater importance placed on fluency in French or English and more discretion awarded to immigration officials in determining adaptability disadvantage applicants from some parts of the world more than others?

With the liberal philosophy in place, the effects of Bill C-44 and other amendments to Canadian immigration law, policy and practice remain to be seen. Will immigration become a more exclusionary practice that further perpetuates racism and discrimination? Or will the Canadian government adopt a leading international role in a more global movement towards the elimination of racial discrimination? Only time will tell.

References

Abella, I. 1982. *None Is Too Many: Canada and the Jews of Europe, 1933–1948.* Toronto: Lester and Orpen Dennys.

Abercrombie, N., S. Hill, and B.S. Turner. 1988. *Dictionary of Sociology.* Markham, Ont.: Penguin Books.

Allahar A. 1989. *Sociology and the Periphery: Theories and Issues.* Toronto: Garamond Press.

———— 1986. "Ideology, Social Order and Social Change." In L. Tepperman, R.J. Richardson (eds.), *The Social World: An Introduction to Sociology.* Toronto: McGraw-Hill Ryerson.

Althusser, L. 1969. *For Marx.* Harmondsworth: Penguin Books.

Baldus, B. 1977. "Social Control in Capitalist Societies: An Examination of the 'Problem of Order' in Liberal Democracies." *Canadian Journal of Sociology* 2(3):247-62.

———— 1975. "The Study of Power: Suggestions for an Alternative." *Canadian Journal of Sociology* 1(2):179-201.

Basran, G.S. 1983. "Canadian Immigration Policies and Theories of Racism." In P.S. Li and B.S. Bolaria (eds.), *Racial Minorities in Canada.* Toronto: Garamond Press.

Beirne, P. and R. Quinney. 1982. "Social Theory and Law." In P. Beirne and R. Quinney (eds.), *Marxism and Law.* New York: John Wiley and Sons.

Bell, S. "Task Force to Track Foreign Criminals to be Made Permanent." *London Free Press*, September 9, 1995:A7.

Birnbaum, N. 1953. "Conflicting Interpretations of the Rise of Capitalism: Marx and Weber." In *The Bobbs-Merill Reprint Series*, #S26:125-141. Originally published in *The British Journal of Sociology*, vol. 4, June 1953.

Bohannan, P. 1973. "The Different Realms of Law." In D. Black and M. Mileski (eds.), *The Social Organization of Law.* New York: Seminar Press.

Bolaria, B.S., and P.S. Li. 1988. *Racial Oppression in Canada.* Toronto: Garamond Press.

Bonacich, E. 1980. "Class Approaches to Ethnicity and Race." *The Insurgent Sociologist* 10(2):9-23.

———— 1976. "Advanced Capitalism and Black/White Race Relations in the United States: A Split Labour Market Interpretation." *American Sociological Review* 41(February):34-51.

———— 1972. "A Theory of Ethnic Antagonism: The Split Labour Market." *American Sociological Review* 37(October):547-59.

Bouhdiba, A. 1981. "Racism and Economic and Social Conditions." In *Racism, Science and Pseudo-Science*—Proceedings of the Symposium to Examine Pseudo-Scientific Theories Invoked to Justify Racism and Racial Discrimination. Athens, March 30 to April 3 1981. UNESCO:125-32.

Burtch, B. 1992. *The Sociology of Law: Critical Approaches to Social Control.* Toronto: Harcourt Brace Jovanovich Canada.

Cain, M. 1982. "The Main Themes in Marx' and Engels' Sociology of Law." In P. Beirne and R. Quinney (eds.), *Marxism and Law.* New York: John Wiley and Sons.

Calliste, A. 1991. "Canada's Immigration Policy and Domestics From the Caribbean: The Second Domestic Scheme." In J. Vorst et al. (eds.), *Race, Class, Gender:*

Bonds and Barriers. Second edition. Toronto: Garamond Press.

Canada. 1992. *House of Commons Debates.* 3rd Session, 34th Parliament, June 22.

Canadian Immigration Act. R.S. 1985, c.1-2, November 1989.

Cappon, P. 1975. "The Green Paper: Immigration as a Tool of Profit." *Canadian Ethnic Studies* 7:50-54.

Caragata, W. 1992c. "Immigration Changes Play to the Right." *Toronto Star*, June 17: A19.

Chambliss, W. 1986. "On Lawmaking." In S. Brickey and E. Comack (eds.), *The Social Basis of Law: Critical Readings in the Sociology of Law.* Toronto: Garamond Press.

——— 1969. *Crime and the Legal Process.* New York: McGraw-Hill.

Collins, H. 1982. *Marxism and Law.* Toronto: Oxford University Press.

Corbett, D. 1957. *Canada's Immigration Policy.* Toronto: University of Toronto Press.

Cotterrell, R. 1992. *Sociology of Law: An Introduction.* Second edition. London: Butterworths.

Cox, O.C. 1948. *Caste, Race and Class.* New York: Modern Reader Paperbacks.

Cox, W. 1995. "Ottawa Changes Rules for Entry." *London Free Press,* November 18: A7.

Davis, A. 1983. *Women, Race and Class.* New York: Vintage Books.

de Silva, A. 1992. *Earnings of Immigrants: A Comparative Analysis.* A study prepared for the Economic Council of Canada. Ottawa: Supply and Services Canada.

Dirks, G. 1977. *Canada's Refugee Policy: Indifference or Opportunism?* Montreal and London: McGill-Queen's University Press.

Dummett, A. 1973. *A Portrait of English Racism.* Harmondsworth: Penguin Books.

Durkheim, E. 1965. *The Elementary Forms of Religious Life.* New York: Free Press.

——— 1964a. *The Rules of Sociological Method.* Glencoe, Ill.: Free Press.

——— 1964b. *The Division of Labour in Society.* Glencoe, Ill.: Free Press.

Economic Council of Canada. 1991a. *New Faces in the Crowd: Economic and Social Impacts of Immigration.* Ottawa: Supply and Services Canada.

——— 1991b. *Economic and Social Impacts of Immigration.* Ottawa: Supply and Services Canada.

Elliot, J.E. and A. Fleras. 1996. *Unequal Relations: An Introduction to Race and Ethnic and Aboriginal Dynamics in Canada.* Second edition. Scarborough: Prentice-Hall Canada.

——— 1992. *Unequal Relations: An Introduction to Race and Ethnic Dynamics in Canada.* Scarborough: Prentice-Hall Canada.

——— 1990. "Immigration and Ethnic Relations in Canada." In P.S. Li (ed.), *Race and Ethnic Relations in Canada.* Toronto: Oxford University Press.

Employment and Immigration Canada. 1991. "Admission to Canada—Immigrants (General)." In *Immigration Manual—Selection and Control, vol.1.* Ottawa: Supply and Services Canada.

Freeman, A. 1982. "Anti-Discrimination Law: A Critical Review." In D. Kairys (ed.), *The Politics of Law: A Progressive Critique.* New York: Pantheon Books.

Friedmann, W. 1959. *Law in a Changing Society.* Berkeley: University of California Press.

Fontana, Joe, MP, London East. 1994. Parliamentary Report. Issue 2, July.

Gallup Report. 1992a. "Economic Difficulties Preoccupy Canadian Public." May 7.

——— 1992b. "Majority Believe Racial Intolerance Has Increased." May 25.

——— 1992c. "Nearly One Half of Public Favours Lower Immigration." June 9.

Giddings, P. 1984. *When and Where I Enter: The Impact of Black Women on Race and Sex in America.* New York: Bantam Books.

Gramsci, A. 1971. *Selections from the Prison Notebooks.* New York: International Publishers.

Green, A. 1976. *Immigration and the Postwar Canadian Economy.* Toronto: Macmillan.

Guillaumin, C. 1980. "The Idea of Race and its Elevation to Autonomous Legal Status." In *Sociological Theories: Race and Colonialism.* Paris: UNESCO.

Hall, S. 1988. "The Toad in the Garden: Thatcherism Among the Theorists." In C. Nelson and L. Grossberg (eds.), *Marxism and the Interpretation of Culture.* Chicago: University of Illinois Press.

Hall, S., C. Critcher, T. Jefferson, J. Clarke, and B. Roberts. 1978. *Policing the Crisis: Mugging, the State, Law and Order.* London: Macmillan.

Harper, T. 1992. "Immigration Plan: Is Canada Getting Meaner?" *Toronto Star,* September 14:A1/A24.

Hawkins, F. 1989. *Critical Years in Immigration: Canada and Australia Compared.* Montreal: McGill-Queen's University Press.

———— 1988. *Canadian Immigration: Public Policy and Public Concern.* Second edition. Montreal: McGill-Queen's University Press.

Henry, F., C. Tator, W. Mattis, and T. Rees. 1995. *The Colour of Democracy: Racism in Canadian Society.* Toronto: Harcourt Brace and Company.

hooks, b. 1981. *Ain't I a Woman: black women and feminism.* Boston: South End Press.

Hopkins, A. 1975. "On the Sociology of Criminal Law." *Social Problems* 22 (June):608-19.

House of Commons. 1992. *Minutes of Proceedings and Evidence of the Legislative Committee on Bill C-86.* Issue 3 (July 28). Issue 4 (July 29). Issue 5 (July 30). Issue 8 (August 12). Issue 10 (September 15).

———— 1991, 1992, 1993. *Minutes of Proceedings and Evidence of the Standing Committee on Labour, Employment and Immigration.* Issue 8 (December 4, 1991; February 6 and 26, 1992). Issue 20 (June 17, 18, 22, and 23, 1992). Issue 25 (February 25, 1993).

Hunt, A. 1991. "Marxism, Law, Legal Theory and Jurisprudence." In P. Fitzpatrick (ed.), *Dangerous Supplements: Resistance and Renewal in Jurisprudence.* Durham: Duke University Press.

———— 1985. "The Ideology of Law: Advances and Problems in Recent Applications of the Concept of Ideology to the Analysis of Law." *Law and Society Review* 19(1):11-37.

———— 1982. "Emile Durkheim: Towards a Sociology of Law." In P. Beirne and R. Quinney (eds.), *Marxism and Law.* New York: John Wiley and Sons.

Immigration Canada. 1993. *Canada's Immigration Law.* Ottawa: Supply and Services Canada.

———— 1992. *Managing Immigration: A Framework for the 1990s.* Ottawa: Supply and Services Canada.

Kallen, E. 1989. *Label Me Human: Minority Rights of Stigmatized Canadians.* Toronto: University of Toronto Press.

Knuttila, M. 1992. *State Theories: From Liberalism to the Challenge of Feminism.* Second edition. Halifax: Fernwood Publishing.

Kopvillem, P. 1990. "Faces from Far Shores: Immigrants Are Testing Canada's Self-Image of Racial Tolerance." *Maclean's* January 1:40.

References

Law Society of Upper Canada. 1993. *Understanding the New Immigration Act—How Bill C-86 Rewrites the Law* (Prepared for program held in Toronto on January 15).

Law Union of Ontario. 1981. *The Immigrant's Handbook*. Montreal: Black Rose Books.

LEI—see House of Commons. *Minutes of Proceedings and Evidence of the Standing Committee on Labour, Employment and Immigration.*

London Free Press. 1994a. "Police Want Answers from Immigration Officials." June 21:A3.

——— 1994b. "Police Want RCMP to Round-Up Dangerous Offenders." June 27:A4.

MacKinnon, C.A. 1987. "Feminism, Marxism, Method and the State: Towards Feminist Jurisprudence." In S. Harding (ed.), *Feminism and Methodology*. Bloomington: Indiana University Press.

——— 1982. "Feminism, Marxism, Method and the State: An Agenda for Theory" *Signs* 7(3):515-44.

Malarek, V. 1987. *Haven's Gate: Canada's Immigration Fiasco*. Toronto: Macmillan.

Manpower and Immigration Canada. 1974. *The Immigration Program*. Ottawa: Information Canada.

Marx, K. 1973. *Grundrisse: Introduction to the Critique of Political Economy*. Harmondsworth: Penguin Books.

——— 1964. *Selected Writings in Sociology and Social Philosophy*. In T.B. Bottomore and M. Rubel (eds.), New York: McGraw-Hill.

Marx, K., and F. Engels. 1986. *The German Ideology*. C.J. Arthur (ed.). New York: International Publishers.

Matas, D. and I. Simon. 1989. *Closing the Doors: The Failure of Refugee Protection*. Toronto: Summerhill National Demographic Review.

McCarthy, S. 1995. "497 Crooks Deported Since Officer Killed." *Toronto Star,* September 9:A14.

McLellan, D. 1986. *Ideology*. Minneapolis: University of Minnesota Press.

Miles, R. 1989. *Racism*. London: Routledge.

——— 1984. "Marxism versus the sociology of 'race relations'?" *Ethnic and Racial Studies* 7(2):217-37.

Miles, R. and A. Phizacklea. 1984. *White Man's Country: Racism in British Politics*. London: Pluto Press.

Minow, M. 1990. *Making All the Difference: Inclusion, Exclusion and American Law*. Ithaca: Cornell University Press.

Mouffe, C. 1988. "Hegemony and New Political Subjects: Towards a Concept of Democracy." In L. Grossberg and C. Nelson (eds.), *Marxism and the Interpretation of Culture*. Chicago: University of Chicago Press.

O'Connor, J. 1973. *The Fiscal Crisis of the State*. New York: St. Martin's Press.

Panitch, L. 1977. "The Role and Nature of the Canadian State." In L. Panitch (ed.), *The Canadian State: Political Economy and Political Power*. Toronto: University of Toronto Press.

Parsons, T. 1951. *The Social System*. New York: Free Press.

Polan, D. 1982. "Towards a Theory of Law and Patriarchy" In D. Kairys (ed.), *The Politics of Law: A Progressive Critique*. New York: Pantheon Books.

Portes, A. 1978. "Migration and Underdevelopment." *Politics and Race* 8(1):1-48.

Reeves, F. 1983. *British Racial Discourse: A Study of British Political Discourse about Race and Race-Related Matters*. Cambridge: Cambridge University Press.

Reimers, D.M., and H. Troper. 1992. "Canadian and American Immigration Policy

Since 1945." In B.R. Chiswick (ed.), *Immigration, Language and Ethnicity*. Washington: The AEI Press

Rejai, M. 1971. "Political Ideology: Theoretical and Comparative Perspectives." In M. Rejai (ed.), *Decline of Ideology?* Chicago: Adline-Atherton.

Rex, J. 1983. *Race Relations and Sociological Theory*. London: Routledge and Kegan Paul.

Samuel, T.J. 1990. "Third World Immigration and Multiculturalism." In S. Halli, F. Trovato and L. Driedger (eds.), *Ethnic Demography: Canadian Immigrant, Racial and Cultural Variations*. Ottawa: Carleton University Press.

Satzewich, V. 1991. "The Contradictions of International Migration." In B. Singh Bolaria (ed.), *Social Issues and Contradictions in Canadian Society*. Toronto: Harcourt Brace Jovanovich Canada.

Sawer, G. 1965. *Law in Society*. Oxford: Clarendon Press.

Silbey, S. 1989. "A Sociological Interpretation of the Relationship Between Law and Society." In R.J. Neuhaus (ed.), *Law and the Ordering of Our Life Together*. Michigan: William B. Eerdmans Publishing.

Silvera, M. 1989. *Silenced*. Toronto: Sister Vision—Black Women and Women of Colour Press.

Simmons, Alan B. 1992. "Canadian Migration in the Western Hemisphere." Paper prepared for the workshop on *Canada's Role in the Hemisphere: Setting the Agenda*. Organized by the North-South Centre, University of Miami, March 27-28.

——— 1990. "'New Wave' Immigrants: Origins and Characteristics." In S. Halli, F. Trovato and L. Driedger (eds.), *Ethnic Demography: Canadian Immigrant, Racial and Cultural Variations*. Ottawa: Carleton University Press.

Simmons, A.B., and K. Keohane. 1992. "Canadian Immigration Policy: State Strategies and the Quest for Legitimacy." *The Canadian Review of Sociology and Anthropology* 29(4):421-52.

Smart, C. 1991. "Feminist Jurisprudence." In P. Fitzpatrick (ed.), *Dangerous Supplements: Resistance and Renewal in Jurisprudence*. Durham: Duke University Press.

Smith, D. 1990a. *The Conceptual Practices of Power: A Feminist Sociology of Knowledge*. Toronto: University of Toronto Press.

——— 1990b. *Texts, Facts and Femininity: Exploring the Relations of Ruling*. London: Routledge.

——— 1987. *The Everyday World as a Problematic: A Feminist Sociology*. Toronto: University of Toronto Press.

Stafford, J. 1990. "A Critical Analysis of Recent Changes in Canadian Immigration Policy." Paper presented in *The Twelfth World Congress of Sociology*, Madrid, July 9-13. Department of Sociology, Lakehead University, Thunder Bay, Ontario, mimeo.

Statutes of Canada.

1992. *Bill C-86: An Act to Amend the Immigration Act* Chapter 49.

1923. *An Act Respecting Chinese Immigration* Chapter 38.

1903. *An Act Respecting and Restricting Chinese Immigration* Chapter 8.

1900. *An Act Respecting and Restricting Chinese Immigration* Chapter 32.

1885. *An Act To Restrict and Regulate Chinese Immigration into Canada* Chapter 71.

Sumner, C. 1982. "The Ideological Nature of Law." In P. Beirne and R. Quinney (eds.), *Marxism and Law*. New York: John Wiley and Sons.

Task Force on Immigration Practices and Procedures. 1981. *Domestic Workers on Employment Authorizations, A Report*. Ottawa: Supply and Services Canada.

Thompson, A. 1993. "Closing the Door." *Toronto Star*, January 13:B1/B7.

Thompson, E.P. 1982. "The Rule of Law." In P. Beirne and R. Quinney (eds.), *Marxism and Law*. New York: John Wiley and Sons.

Toronto Star. 1992a. "Legislation Would Tell Immigrants Where to Live." June 17:A1/A18.

———. 1992b. "Ottawa's New Immigration Rules *Blame the Victims* Critics Charge." June 18:A3.

Turk, A. 1976. "Law as a Weapon in Social Conflict." *Social Problems* 23(3):276-91.

Vienneau, D. 1990. "Rights Chief Slams Rise in Racism, Intolerance." *Toronto Star*, March 30:A1.

"Voices of Canada—Maclean's/CTV Poll" 1993. *Maclean's* January 4:42-45.

Weber, M. 1968. *Economy and Society*. New York: Bedminster Press.

——— 1964. *The Theory of Social and Economic Organization*. Glencoe: Free Press.

——— 1958. *The Protestant Ethic and the Spirit of Capitalism*. New York: Charles Scribner's Sons.

——— 1954. *On Law in Economy and Society*. E. Shils and M. Rheinstein (trans.). Cambridge: Harvard University Press.

Whitaker, R. 1987. *Double Standard: The Secret History of Canadian Immigration*. Toronto: Lester and Orpen Dennys.

Wood, N. 1993. "Immigration: A Reluctant Welcome." *Maclean's* January 4:26-27.

Young, M. 1995a. *Canada's Refugee Status Determination System (Background Paper)*. Ottawa: Library of Parliament Research Branch.

——— 1995b. *Bill C-44: An Act to Amend the Immigration Act and the Citizenship Act (Legislative Summary)*. Ottawa: Library of Parliament Research Branch.

——— 1994. *Canada's Immigration Program (Background Paper)*. Ottawa: Library of Parliament Research Branch.

——— 1992. *Bill C-86: An Act to Amend the Immigration Act (Legislative Summary)*. Ottawa: Library of Parliament Research Branch.

——— 1991a. *Canada's Immigration Program (Background Paper)*. Ottawa: Library of Parliament Research Branch—Law and Government Division, February.

——— 1991b. *Canada's Refugee Determination System (Background Paper)*. Ottawa: Library of Parliament Research Branch, February.

Zeitlin, I. 1987. *Ideology and the Development of Sociological Theory*. Englewood Hills, NJ: Prentice-Hall.

769012